THE INSIDE PATH TO BETTER GOLF

THE INSIDE PATH TO BETTER GOLF

BY PETER KOSTIS
with Larry Dennis

A GOLF DIGEST BOOK

Published by NYT Special Services, Inc.
A New York Times Company
5520 Park Avenue
Box 395
Trumbull, Connecticut 06611-0395

Trade book distributed by:
Pocket Books
1230 Avenue of the Americas
New York, New York 10020

ISBN: 0-671-72311-1
Library of Congress: 82-80148
9   8   7   6   5
Manufactured in the
United States of America

Cover and book design
by Dorothy Geiser.

CREDITS

Photography

All photographs by Steve Szurlej except pp. 13 and 179, Larry Petrillo; p. 16 (left), Lester Nehamkin; pp. 16 (right) and 17, Will Hertzberg; p. 19 (left), United Press International; p. 19 (right), Chuck Brenkus and p. 39, Associated Press.

Illustration

All illustrations by Elmer Wexler.

TABLE OF CONTENTS

ON THE MAKING OF A BOOK.... AND A TEACHER

On the day we were to begin work on this book, Peter Kostis arrived at my hotel room laden with a stack of books under one arm and a briefcase full of handwritten outline material under the other.

"Are you prepared?" I asked, jokingly.

"I'm prepared," Kostis replied, seriously.

And so for four days we slugged it out in front of a tape recorder, in the hotel room and on the practice tee, Peter explaining and demonstrating while I questioned. It is a measure of the Kostis approach to teaching that each of my questions, no matter how ill-conceived, was thoughtfully considered. Sometimes a change in tack resulted. For golf instruction—or any other kind, for that matter—to be effective, there must first be communication. If you don't understand it, you can't benefit from it. That, as Kostis well knows, is especially critical when you are trying to learn from the pages of a book.

We have slugged it out for more than a year since, virtually to the day this is being written. There was, for example, a painstaking photo session at Broken Sound C.C. in Boca Raton, Fla., highlighted—if that's the word—by a day-long battle with a crane. Kostis had it moved laboriously, often inches at a time, so photographer Steve Szurlej could shoot at exactly the angle Peter wanted for the overhead pictures you'll see in the book.

And when the manuscript was more than half-completed, Kostis decided a book that was meant to be simple had grown too complex, so he reorganized the whole thing to make it simple again.

That should come as no surprise to anyone who knows Peter Kostis. It certainly did not surprise me. I met Peter in 1973, when he was the head professional at The Hamlet in Delray Beach, Fla., and in the years since have watched him grow in his profession. He has learned much from an early and continuing association with Jim Flick and Bob Toski and from the other teachers with whom he is involved as a member of the Golf Digest Professional Instruction Staff and as a head teacher in the Golf Digest Instruction Schools. Today they learn as much, if not more, from him.

Four years ago Kostis made invaluable contributions to Toski and Flick's best-selling book, "How to Become a Complete Golfer." At the time, Toski said, "In 10 years Peter Kostis will be the best teacher in the world." That subjective judgment eventually must be left up to those who know best—the students—but right now Kostis, at the relatively tender age of 35, surely is in the running.

It was my privilege to work with Toski and Flick on that book, as I have been privileged to work with many of the game's superstar teachers and players on books and instruction articles for Golf Digest. None has brought more thorough preparation and dedication to the task than Kostis.

It is a by-product of his background. He brings to his work the analytical mind of a graduate engineer, which he is; the competitive instincts of a football quarterback, which he was; and the skill and knowledge of a golfer with Tour potential had he chosen to go that route. He is an expert club designer and a student of physiology, kinesiology and fitness, not to mention psychology. A few years ago he banished red meat permanently from his diet and lost 40 unwanted pounds. Two years ago he quit smoking cold turkey, using self-hypnosis to convince himself that cigarettes made him sick. The last time I was in his Boca Raton residence, I found him hanging from his heels, which he does 20 minutes a day to help correct an ailing back and accomplish other good things for his body.

"I'm half an inch taller since I started doing it," he announced.

He brings this same discipline to his teaching; but it is a discipline that results not in dogmatism but in never-ending research to find out what in the world is going on. As far as Kostis is concerned, there is no right or wrong in the golf swing but rather what works for you, as you will learn in this book. To find what that is and to present it as simply as possible is his *raison d'être*. And he has been able to do that for amateurs at all levels and Tour professionals alike.

Tom Kite, the Tour's leading money-winner, Vardon Trophy winner and the golf writers' Player of the Year in 1981, has been a Toski disciple for nine years. In the process, he has become a fan of Kostis and of this book.

"I've worked with Peter quite a bit, and I really like his theories," Kite says. "I like what he is trying to do and I like the simplicity that he puts into teaching the game. He has written a book that definitely can help people. He teaches you how to draw the ball, which is what the majority of players on Tour do. He gives you a definite theory of how to play the game without throwing out so much knowledge that it confuses you."

Peter Kostis

Peter's ordeal—and mine—has indeed resulted in a remarkable book that not only presents a keen insight into the golf swing and what it's about but, in a unique four-stage development program, actually tells you how to build that swing from the ground up.

"I want to make people understand that there is more than one way to accomplish an effective golf swing," Kostis says, "that they don't have to pursue the common golf cliche's to find that swing. And I want them to understand that developing a golf swing requires stages of learning, one building on the other. If a person approaches it that way, he can build a solid, effective swing, one that will last. Finally, they must understand that no one ever gets it forever. The game of golf requires constant adjustment and alteration. By understanding the learning process, they should be able to help themselves when things go bad. They can go back and reconstruct the swing."

We have been warned to beware of Greeks bearing gifts, and this Greek's gift is no exception. Kostis is firm in the belief that there is no magic carpet to success. In this book he gives you the opportunity to learn to play better golf. Whether you do will depend on the time and effort you are willing to devote to the task. But if you take advantage of the tools he offers, the way certainly will be made easier.

Larry Dennis
Huntington, Connecticut
May, 1982

CHAPTER · 1

THE PERFECT SWING IS THE ONE THAT WORKS FOR YOU

The origins of golf appear to be lost in time and probably will remain so. But, one thing is certain—wherever and whenever the first person took that first swipe with whatever kind of club at whatever kind of object in an attempt to propel it toward a target, ever since there has been the search for the perfect swing.

During each era in golf the masses have looked to the successful golfers of the day as the ideal "models" to be emulated. Bobby Jones, Sam Snead, Ben Hogan, Arnold Palmer, Jack Nicklaus and Tom Watson are just a few.

But Bobby Jones' swing bore little resemblance to Jack Nicklaus', and Ben Hogan's swing bears absolutely no resemblance to either one. That doesn't make one right and the others wrong. It just makes them different in appearance. But they are identical in the most important consideration. All three swings consistently produced winning shots.

Golf, after all, is a game of shots. But consider that the best players in history had good days and bad days and that on their best days they mis-struck more shots than they hit perfectly. The hunt, then, should not be for a perfect swing and perfect shots, but for an effective swing that produces playable shots the greatest percentage of the time.

Rarely can any swing model, no matter how ideal, be reproduced 100 percent by any individual. So it should be a comfort to realize that a successful and rewarding golf game doesn't require a perfect swing. You can develop a swing which may look different than Tom Watson's but will work better for you.

I believe there are two constants in every effective full swing—*a swing path that approaches the ball from inside the target line and a swing motion that efficiently produces clubhead speed.*

Satisfying those criteria lets you

achieve the one thing you need to play golf well—shots that are *long* enough to reach the target in the required number of strokes and that are *accurate* enough to end up somewhere near that target.

How you do this is an individual matter. All the golf ball knows is impact. It does not care how you use your body, so long as it allows the clubface to arrive at impact in position to produce the best possible ball flight.

Bob Toski is naturally quick. His body moves quickly, so he can use the rapid movement of his hands, arms and legs to produce sufficient clubhead speed.

Julius Boros does not move quickly. He does not have inherent body quickness or arm speed. Instead, he gets his clubhead speed from excessive hand action—excessive for some perhaps, but not for Julius' strong and talented hands.

Al Geiberger is a slender, flexible person neither excessively strong nor quick. He can make a long, full swing without his left heel coming very far off the ground.

Nicklaus doesn't have the flexibility

16

Three different-looking "modern" swings—they all get the job done

The swings of Arnold Palmer (left), Tom Watson (middle) and Jack Nicklaus all embody basic modern principles but are dissimilar in appearance. Each, however, allows the player to best utilize his physical characteristics to make winning golf shots.

that Geiberger has. So he creates artificial flexibility by releasing his left heel, allowing it to lift markedly on the backswing so he can make the full turn he wants.

Arnold Palmer is a wonderful example of a player who uses his great strength to advantage. He does not have a great deal of flexibility, so he creates his clubhead speed with tremendous hand, arm and shoulder strength.

Tom Watson potentially may be the best of all because he has all the assets—strength, flexibility and quickness—and has built a swing that takes advantage of each.

If there is a "secret" to becoming the golfer we all want to be, the players just mentioned discovered it long ago. They all built a sound swing technique that took advantage of their physical assets while compensating for their weaknesses. Had Boros tried to copy Toski, or had Nicklaus emulated Palmer, they would not have achieved nearly as much as they have.

Thus, since only the club has to be in a specific position, and that's only at impact, we can use our bodies in many different ways to swing the club on the correct inside path to the ball. Most people are in a mess because they are mixing apples and oranges—trying to match someone else's techniques and preferences to themselves. The great players have avoided this problem like the plague.

The solution is to properly blend a sound swing technique that matches your physical talents and to spend enough time to develop a measure of consistency. Ben Hogan has often been quoted as saying his triumphs in golf were 15 percent talent, with the remaining 85 percent resulting from the time he spent working and the technique he developed during that work. The three T's—*Talent, Time and Technique*—then become the keystones of success.

Another way to understand the necessary individuality of the golf swing is to study its evolution from classic to modern. Again, I'm not saying one is right and the other wrong. Just because something was done in 1850 or 1920 doesn't make it wrong any more than something is right just because it is being done today. Both types of swing, and all the modifications in between, existed for a purpose.

I do think there are things players using the classic swing did that the average player of today ought to consider incorporating in his own swing. Many amateurs are unduly influenced by the example of top modern golfers. Often they are making a mistake to copy the tour star, for various reasons,

including different physical characteristics, the amount of time they can devote to the game and their particular stage of development.

Bearing in mind that both classic and modern golf swings are viable today, let's briefly compare the two:

The classic grip is more in the fingers, which promotes wrist flexion. The modern grip is more palm-oriented, more neutral or palms-facing, with less flexing of the wrists.

The classic player tended to get his body and clubface aimed to the right, with the result that he hit mostly right-to-left shots. The good modern player—the top amateur and tour professional—sets his body and clubface more squarely to the target or to the left, resulting in more of a left-to-right shot pattern.

The classic swinger favored positioning the ball toward his right foot—slightly forward of center with the woods and long irons, center with the 5-iron and right of center with the shorter irons. This suited his closed body position and enabled him to better hit the right-to-left shot with a lower flight of the ball. The modern player tends to position the ball off his left heel, plus or minus a ball-width or so, for every shot. This helps produce the higher, left-to-right flight that he wants.

The footwork in the classic and modern swing is different. In the classic swing, the left heel came way off the ground on the backswing and the right heel came way off the

"Classic" and "modern" swings—
they both get the job done

The classical, flowing swing of Bobby Jones
(left) and the modern, more compact swing
used by Ben Hogan both produced successful
shots and astounding tournament records.

ground on the follow-through. Basically this was because the earliest golfers wore heavy clothing that restricted their movement. They found that by lifting the heels and turning the body more going back and forward they could create more freedom. The good modern player, who is bigger, taller, stronger, more flexible and wears non-restrictive clothing, can swing his arms fully enough that the heels don't have to come off the ground as much.

The classic swing placed a greater emphasis on hand action. Arms were more tied to the body, the right elbow tucked in on the backswing and the left elbow tucked in on the follow-through, so hand action was needed to create clubhead speed. In the modern swing there is more arm freedom, the arms doing more to control the swing, and correspondingly less emphasis on the hands.

The classic swing was more rotary and vertical with very little lateral action—the "turn in a barrel" concept. The swing was more around-to-around and the path to the ball more inside-out, the blade squaring up to hook the ball. This accommodated not only the whippier shafts in use then, but also produced the low, running-type shot needed to play the firm Scottish and English courses in the windy weather common there.

The modern player, who uses stiffer shafts and needs to hit the ball higher, especially on the lush courses in the United States, has a swing that is more lateral and vertical with less rotary ac-

tion. His swing is more down the line and the ball starts straighter to the target with less curvature.

All this to reiterate my belief that there is more than one way to skin a cat as far as the golf swing goes. My purpose in this book is to help each reader find the way that works the best for him. I propose to do this as follows:

First, I will explain the fundamentals related to impact conditions and to the basic preparation for making a swing.

Then, I will put you through a four-stage process designed to nurture the effective swing that is uniquely yours. Here we will progress through what I call:

•**The first swing,** which is the swinging of the hands and clubhead from the arms;

•**The second swing,** the swinging of the arms from the shoulders;

•**The pivot** of the body that supports those two swings, and finally,

•**The timing** that will allow you to put it all together—swinging with the correct speed-producing muscles on the correct inside path.

Following this very specific—and intensive—swing-building process, we will step back and examine the results we're getting. Essentially, this will be a chance to do some trouble-shooting in case you are unintentionally sabotaging your learning process because you are misled by any of the numerous instructional myths prevalent in golf today, or simply by overusing or underusing a certain part of your body.

Finally, we will show you how our full-swing knowledge applies equally as well to the short game—approach shots, sand shots and putting.

Once you understand the concepts in this book, and then apply them through diligent practice, I feel sure you will develop a golf swing that produces the good shots I discussed earlier—shots that are longer and straighter than you've ever been able to strike before. It will be a swing that can carry you far along the road to better, more enjoyable golf.

CHAPTER · 2

THE FIVE FUNDAMENTALS OF IMPACT

WHAT YOU NEED TO KNOW BEFORE YOU CAN BUILD A BETTER SWING

Every shot ever hit has been influenced by five fundamentals:

1. The **path** of the club through impact,

2. The **speed** at which the clubhead is moving,

3. The **position of the clubface** at impact,

4. The **angle** at which the clubhead approaches the ball, and

5. The **point on the clubface** where contact occurs.

The fact that these fundamentals, and these fundamentals only, determine where the ball goes explains why so many productive golf swings can appear so different.

All five fundamentals interact to produce the ball flight, and it is, at best, dangerous to analyze each fundamental on its own simply because a golf shot is made up of so many dimensions. Distance and direction are obvious dimensions, but there is also ball spin, trajectory and curvature. All must be considered. For teaching pur-

poses, I maintain that the *starting* direction of the ball is determined by the swing path and the *curving* direction of the ball results from the position of the clubface relative to the swing path. Clubface position also has an influence on the starting direction, as does clubface speed and point of contact, but I've found that equating path with starting direction and clubface position with curvature has helped my pupils from a practical standpoint.

Before you can begin developing *your* correct swing, I want you to understand the process every good player goes through in preparing for a successful shot.

1. Identify the desired ball flight.

2. Understand the necessary impact conditions to produce the ball flight.

3. Identify the swing shape that will create impact properly.

4. Decide how to use your body in making the swing motion.

If you are to play with purpose and plan for success, then, consciously or

The inside-to-inside
swing—down the line

When the club swings on the correct path, it starts straight back and gradually moves up and inside on the backswing. The return to the ball is on a path inside that of the backswing path, the club approaching the ball from inside the target line, traveling briefly along that line through impact, then moving back inside the line on the follow-through.

subconsciously, you must go through this four-step process. Unfortunately, most golfers can't prepare in this fashion because they don't understand what happens during impact in a good golf shot.

The speed of the clubhead at impact has the single greatest influence on the *distance* the ball travels, while the angle of approach of the clubhead has the most effect on the trajectory of the shot. An on-center hit—when ball and clubface contact each other "squarely"—influences all aspects of the ball flight. But the greatest effect of on-center hits is the consistency they give to shots.

1. CLUBHEAD PATH
Swing from Inside to Banish the Slice

Now let's look at the correct swing path in greater detail. The club starts straight back along the target line and gradually moves up and inside. It continues around the body and up until it is in position at the top of the backswing. From here the club should take a path back to the ball that keeps it inside of the path it took going back. While this is the ideal overall swing shape, it is important to remember that the only thing the golf ball understands is the direction or path the club is moving *at impact*. The ideal path through impact is one on which the club travels from inside the target line as it approaches the ball, travels directly along the line during impact and swings back inside the line again on the follow-through. That's known as an inside-to-inside swing, and it is ideal for a number of reasons.

Based on my observation of thousands of students, I'd estimate that 85 percent of the golfers in the world slice the ball, or curve it to the right of the starting direction. Of those, three-quarters are pull slicers, which means that they swing on an out-to-in path, starting the ball to the left of their aim and slicing it weakly to the right. They get an early rotation of the body on the forward swing and strike down at a steep angle, hitting pop-ups with the driver and digging deep divots with the irons. A common characteristic of the slicer is a short, choppy follow-through, very low and very much around the body, usually as he falls back onto his right side.

When a slice or a pull occurs, golfers frequently say, "I got over it." That's wrong. You don't get *over* the ball, you just get *outside* the ball. The right side of your body gets outside the left side, producing the out-to-in swing path and the resulting weak ball flight.

The most important by-product of an *inside* path is that you eliminate the weak slice and can hook the ball to the target. With an inside path, the ball will start either at the target or to the right of the target. If your swing path is more in-to-out, then coming at the ball from inside with the clubhead turning over through impact will de-loft the club, giving you a lower ball flight and a more aggressive, distance-producing right-to-left shape to your shots. A study in Golf Digest magazine has proved, at least to my satisfaction, that with a driver swinging at the 85-90 miles-an-hour speed generated by a normal decent player, a ball that is curving slightly right-to-left will travel at least 17 yards farther than one curving in the other direction. The difference is probably even greater when all the other variables are figured in.

I know that in many books and articles written by tour players they say that fading the ball in a left-to-right shape is the more consistent way to play. That's because all these players, whether instinctively or through instruction, grew up hooking the ball. I'm sure that, at some point in his life, every good striker of the ball had to fight a severe hook that kept getting him into trouble. So in his later stages of development he guards against the hook—through positioning of the clubface, a less active rotation of the clubhead or by whatever means—to achieve more consistency.

Well, that's fine for him. But to most players, who have never hooked the ball with any measure of success or who don't have the clubhead speed to get the distance they want and need, the left-to-right shot is the kiss of death. If you are to achieve your potential as a golfer, you must learn to correctly hook the ball. After you can do that, you can learn to control the amount of hook in your shots.

The inside swing path to the ball helps in two other ways. The more inside to inside, or circular, you make your swing path, the more clubhead speed you can generate. You can swing the clubhead faster in a circle than you can in a straight line. The simple function of centrifugal (outward pulling) and centripetal (inward pulling) force dictates that.

Clubhead speed is developed through a system of levers. On the backswing an angle is created between the clubshaft and the arms and another is formed between the arms and the shoulders. On the forward swing, the releasing or straightening of these angles in the proper sequence and at the proper time creates the speed. You can't swing the clubhead very fast by using your arms while keeping your hands immobile, and you can barely move it at all by turning only your shoulders without any arm action.

Swinging from the inside promotes containment of these angles—especially the shaft-arm angle—until the moment they can be released and do the most good through impact. If you are coming into the ball from outside your target line, the angle must be dissipated prematurely. This has to happen with an outside-to-inside swing path if you are to make contact. If you contained the angle with that kind of path, you would swing right across the top of the ball. The releasing of the shaft-arm angle too soon and from the outside is what is commonly referred to as "casting."

Swinging to the ball from the inside also produces a shallower angle of approach, which lets you strike the ball more solidly and gives your shot a better trajectory than if you come down on the ball from the outside with a steeper angle and a more glancing blow.

The golf swing requires the proper blending of three different actions— *lateral, vertical* and *rotary.* The swing goes back and forth—lateral. The swing goes up and down—vertical. And the swing goes, to a certain extent, around your body—rotary. Your arms and hands are the only parts of your body that can accomplish all these actions. Your lower body can move laterally and in a rotary fashion, but certainly not vertically. Your shoulders can rotate and can even move laterally, in a sense, but they can't move vertically if you are to have any chance of striking an effective shot. Only the hands and arms can move in all three ways, which is why you should trust them to control your swing, providing support with the rest of your body.

Most bad swing paths are the result of failure to keep the movement of the body under control. When shoulders and hips create excessive rotary action, they force the swing to the outside because the momentum of the body overtakes the motion of the arms. The most critical point in the swing at which to control the body and, as a result, the swing path has to be the change of direction from backswing to downswing. At this point it is an absolute necessity that the first move-

The inside-to-inside swing—overhead

This view clearly shows the forward swing coming from inside the target line, the club traveling along that line through impact, then swinging back inside on the follow-through.

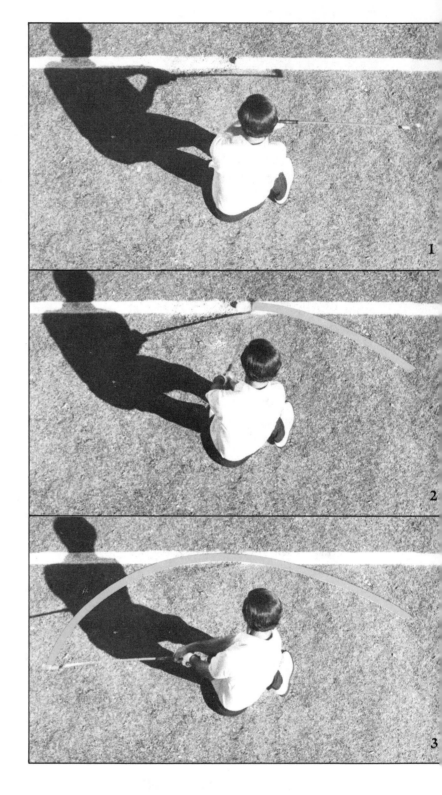

ment of the downswing be downward and forward, *not* outward and around. The rotary action of the body must be contained to allow the club to start downward. If the body releases too quickly and starts unwinding before the club has moved inward and downward, you can be pretty well assured of striking the ball from the outside.

Technically, a correct golf swing is actually two swings: the swinging of the hands and clubhead from the arms at the wrists and the swinging of the arms from the shoulders. This double swinging action is supported by the pivot or turning of your body that allows you to swing into the ball on the correct inside path.

The free-swinging motion created by your hands and arms is the foundation of a good swing path. The hands and arms determine the path on which they will move the club. The feet, legs and the rest of the body pivot and move to provide support to that swinging motion.

2. CLUBHEAD SPEED
Use "Speed Muscles" Not "Support Muscles" to Make It Happen

In watching new golfers hit balls for the first time, it is obvious that their first goal is to make halfway decent contact with the ball and then to get it in the air. Until this is accomplished, the motion of the swing usually is reasonably under control. But once contact and air time have been achieved, players get more aggressive, even violent, because distance enters the picture. No one is ever satisfied with his golf swing until he gets a sufficient amount of distance. It is generally at this point in a player's development that he faces his biggest stumbling block.

To avoid that block, you must understand that distance comes from clubhead speed. The proper creation of clubhead speed allows the other impact factors to be controlled.

The majority of persons who come to me for lessons are searching for distance without this understanding. They have an abundance of effort, but it isn't doing them any good because of an absence of correct technique. They need clubhead speed, but their laboring to muscle the ball not only costs them control but inhibits the very speed they are attempting to produce.

When I get these students to swing the club with the correct muscles and on the proper path and they feel *real* speed, the reaction usually is, "My gosh, I didn't *swing* at that!" Nothing could be further from the truth. In actuality, they were *swinging* for the first time in their lives instead of *hitting*. The feeling of ease that accompanies this swinging motion is always startling when compared to forcing power and distance with the parts of the body that can't produce speed.

The best analogy I can use is the gearshift mechanism in your automobile. First gear is a powerful gear, but it is not a very fast gear. You can drive from Boston to Washington in first gear and get there, but it will take you a long time and you may burn up your transmission along the way. That's the way most persons play golf—in first gear, with their bodies laboring and chugging along. Their golf swings have a lot of effort with little speed. When they don't hit the ball far enough because of this lack of speed, they simply stomp down harder on the accelerator, putting more effort into it. But they haven't changed the gear ratio, so they haven't accomplished anything except to waste more effort and burn themselves up.

Creating proper speed is like shifting into second, third and finally fourth gear. In fourth gear, your car seems to move effortlessly and quickly. Your engine doesn't have much power in fourth gear. You can't take off from a dead stop in that gear, because there isn't enough power to move the weight of the car. But you have a lot of speed. In golf, power does not produce speed, but speed can produce the power you need for distance in your shots.

As I said earlier, clubhead speed is the result of a lever system between the hands and arms, the arms and the shoulders, the shoulders and hips, the hips and knees, the knees and feet. All parts have a function, as do all the gears in your car's transmission. The secret is to get all the parts working properly so you can shift your swing into high gear. If the speed muscles don't produce speed, then the bigger, slower support muscles will overwork to try to create power. Usually the rotary action of the shoulders and hips will increase, which means you not only don't get the speed you want but you also increase your chances of swinging on an incorrect outside path.

Which muscles are the speed muscles and which are the support muscles? Try this experiment for me. Flap one of your hands as fast as you can. Next swing an arm back and forth as fast as you can. Now stand on one leg and swing the other back and forth as fast as possible. Finally, rotate your shoulders with as much speed as you can muster. Which parts of your body can you move the fastest?

The hands, of course, followed by the arms, with the legs lagging well behind and the shoulders coming in a very poor last. Ergo, your hands and arms are your greatest speed producers and should be used to create your clubhead speed.

There is one very important fact to understand in applying the previous exercises to the golf swing. It has to do with the weights of the clubs and balls we use. Small muscles can move small or light objects, while bigger muscles are required to move bigger or heavier objects. A golf ball weighs 1.62 ounces and a club weighs somewhere between 11 and 18 ounces. Compare this with a baseball bat that weighs well over 30 ounces and you can see how light the equipment we use for golf really is. It is this lightness of equipment that allows the small muscles of the hands and arms to create the rapid movement of the golf club. As the speed of the clubhead increases and its effective weight also increases as a result of the forces working on it, the bigger muscles will be called on to provide support for the smaller muscles. To summarize, the smaller, quicker-moving muscles should create the speed in the swing, while the larger, slower muscles provide the support to control the motion.

Understanding that the hands and arms create the speed of the clubhead is important, but learning *how* it is done is even more important. Let me draw some parallels between the throwing action of a baseball player and the swinging action of a golfer. If you examine closely the hand and wrist action in a proper throwing motion, you will find three distinct movements: first, the hand hinges at the wrist in the backward motion; then it unhinges in the forward motion (this is commonly referred to as the "release"); *but* the hand also will rehinge after the release of the ball. In other words, the wrists allow three actions . . . *hinge, unhinge,* then *rehinge.* If you were to try to throw the ball with only two of the three actions, you would reduce your ability to create speed by at least 50 percent.

The hands must do the same thing in the golf swing. They hinge to create an angle between the shaft and lead arm in the backswing, unhinge to release that angle going forward and, finally, rehinge to recreate that shaft-arm angle after impact.

But the hands and wrists can't do it all. Referring back to the throwing action, you will further notice that the hinging at the wrist, allowing hand speed, is supported by the shoulder socket, which allows the arm to swing and carry the hand and wrist action through a longer range of motion. This adds one more lever to the system. This same action should occur in the golf swing. The hands swing the clubhead, while the arms swing the hands resulting in a two-swing, two-lever system that results in what my colleague Bob Toski calls effortless power instead of powerless effort!

3. CLUBFACE POSITION
"Slam the Door" Through Impact

The flight of the ball has two basic directional components, the starting direction and the curving direction. As mentioned earlier, I relate the starting direction to the path of the swing. That being the case, at least from a practical viewpoint, then the curvature of the golf ball results from the position of the clubface relative to the swing path at impact. If you are one of those players who doesn't curve the ball very much because you can't create enough speed in your swing, then the starting direction of your shots will probably be determined more by clubface than swing path.

A clubface position pointing to the right of the swing path at impact will cause the ball to curve to the right or slice. When the clubface is looking left of the swing path, the ball must curve left or hook. There will be no sideways curvature of the ball when the clubface and swing path are looking in the same direction at impact.

Discussing the relationship between path and clubface is akin to talking about the chicken and the egg—which came first? Does the rotation of the clubface react to the swing path, or does the swing path serve to complement the rotation of the clubface? There can be arguments for both viewpoints, but all that really has to happen is for the swing path and clubface to complement each other.

There are only three ball flights that can find the target from any particular aim. When the path is left of the target, then the clubface must be open to allow the ball to curve back to the target. The opposite is true for a path that is right of your aim—a closed clubface position is needed to curve the ball to the target.

Let's examine the movement of the clubface that would provide the proper companion to an inside-to-inside swing path. On the takeaway, the clubface should start rotating as soon as the clubhead starts to move off the target line. It is in this critical area that clubface errors result in having to make a series of compensations during the rest of the swing. *Keeping the clubface square to the target too long will result in a closed to open swing.* A good checkpoint is to have the toe of the club pointing to the sky when it's approximately waist high. A simple exercise that will let you feel this rotation is to extend

The nine possible flights of the ball

This diagram shows the only nine directions the ball can travel in flight, with variations, of course. Depending on the juxtaposition of swing path and clubface position, the ball can (A) start left and hook farther left, start left and continue straight left or start left and slice to the right; (B) start straight and hook left, start straight and continue straight or start straight and slice right; (C) start right and hook left, start right and continue straight right or start right and slice farther to the right. Obviously the only playable shot shapes are A-3, B-2 and C-1.

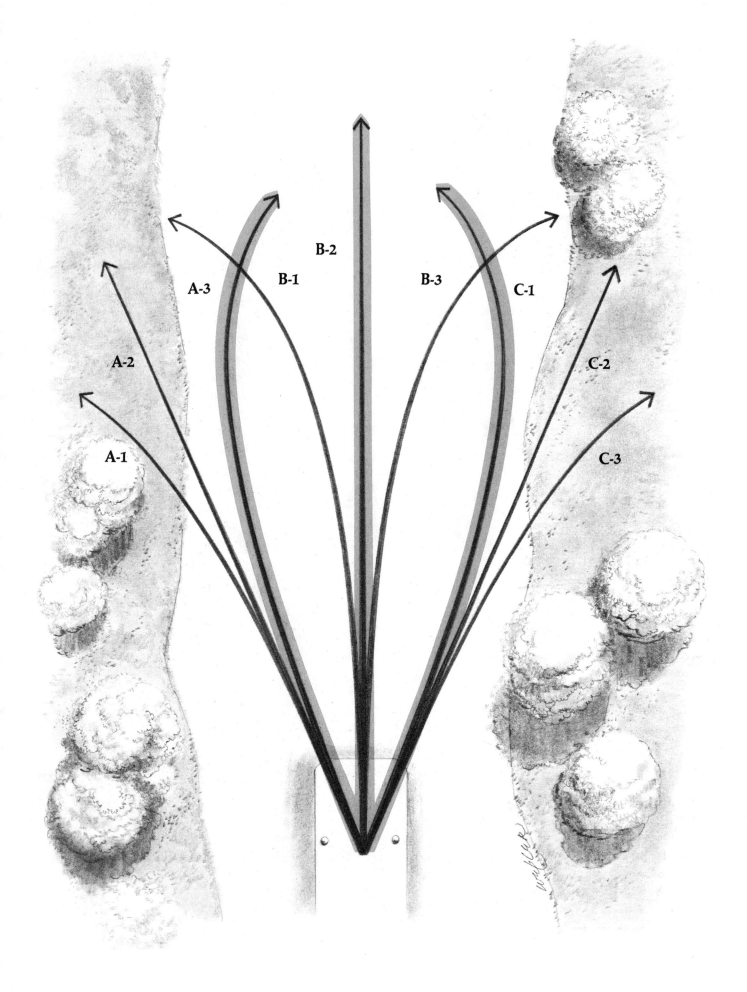

At waist height, make sure toe points to the sky

To make sure you are starting the club away properly, check that the toe of the club is pointing to the sky when it is about waist high on the backswing.

your right hand and arm in front of you as it would be at address without a club, then swing your arm to the right and make sure your thumb points skyward while the palm faces toward the target line at the waist-high position. The player who resists this rotation of the clubface in the first part of the backswing will find that there will be an excessive amount of rotation during the last part. This is the worst place in the swing to try to control the rotation of the clubface. As the saying goes, "Out of sight, out of mind." Once the club is behind you, your ability to sense the position of clubface is greatly reduced.

At the top of the backswing the clubface should be set in the correct position to allow the proper offensive movement during the forward swing. If the face of the club points skyward, then the position is referred to as closed. When the face is looking at the target line and the toe of the club is pointed down, the position is called open. The square or neutral position is when the plane of the clubface is parallel to the plane of the swing. During

Keep clubface square to the swing plane

The ideal position of the clubface at the top of the swing is when the plane of the face is parallel to the plane of the swing (A). If the face is looking to the sky, the club is closed (B). If the face is looking at the target line and the toe is pointing to the ground, the club is open (C).

34

the past few years it has become fashionable to insist on a flat left wrist at the top of the backswing. The wrist position should never dictate the clubface position. Rather, the desired position of the clubface should determine the necessary wrist position. Depending on the grip you use, your wrist position could be flat, cupped or somewhere in between.

The offensive movement I referred to earlier can be visualized by relating to the motion of a swinging door. The toe of the club is akin to the edge of the door that is free swinging, while the heel of the club relates to the edge of the door near the hinges. To be able to slam the door with some force and speed you must first open the door. This may sound ridiculous, but you can't close a door that's already shut, and that is what so many golfers are trying to do. Just as a door can be moved faster when you're closing it, your clubhead speed can be increased if the clubface is closing or turning over through impact.

The phrase "over through impact" should be explained further. In the ideal movement through impact, the toe of the club should be catching up to the heel, squaring up, if you will, at the point of contact with the ball. Immediately after impact the toe of the club should pass the heel. When this happens you will feel that your right hand and arm have crossed over the left hand and arm. To get a better picture of and feel for this move, extend your club at shoulder level in front of your body. The clubhead will be at eye level, the toe pointing straight up. As you swing the club back and around you while maintaining the same plane, you should notice the clubface has rotated and is now facing skyward. On the forward swing the toe of the club will rotate over the heel so that in the follow-through the face is pointing to the ground. As you keep swinging the club back and forth, notice that the shaft maintains a constant plane or path. Even though the clubface is rotating 180 degrees, the path of the swing is staying the same. This is a very important observation, because it can help prevent possible confusion between turning the club over through impact as opposed to swinging the club around through impact. More about that later.

Again, swing the club like a baseball bat and notice that the rotation of the club comes largely from the rotation of the hands and arms. Clubface rotation is and should be independent of the rotation of the body. Golfers who equate the rotation of the body with clubface rotation inevitably start swinging the club to the left too soon on the forward swing—so soon, in fact, that the path of the swing eventually ends up outside-in. That's why there are a lot of golfers who can swing the club to the left with the clubface looking left, or swing the club to the right with the club looking right, but there are so few who can swing the club down the line of play with the face looking at the target.

4. ANGLE OF APPROACH
Come Into Ball Like Soccer-Style Kicker

Ever been on the first tee with a group you've never played with before? There you are, wondering how much to wager and especially how many shots you'll have to give. What can you do to get some sort of edge?

My advice is to watch everyone's practice swings. If anyone takes a divot while swinging the driver, double the bets with that person. The player whose practice swing lightly brushes the grass or better yet touches nothing—beware!

I say this because of the fourth factor of impact, the angle of approach of the clubhead. Simply defined, the angle of approach of the club is the angle in relation to horizontal at which the club arrives at impact with the ball. It can be steep or shallow—descending, level or ascending—and from the inside or the outside.

I wish I had a dollar for every time I've seen someone tee the ball three-quarters of an inch in the air in preparation for the first shot of the round, then take a big practice swing and rip out a piece of turf about 8 inches long. In fact, I've been to some courses where the greens committee has a sign prominently posted on the first tee— "No Practice Swings Allowed!" The game of golf has sometimes been referred to as a game of opposites. That may be, but having the ball *up* in the air and swinging *down* on it doesn't make sense. Of course, neither does

having the ball down in the grass and swinging up to get the ball airborne.

This misunderstanding and misuse of the angle of approach in the swing has kept many players from achieving their potentials. Probably the most common, and most damaging, error I see is a player trying to get under the ball with an iron club to get it airborne. This action is instinctive with beginners, probably because the shorter, more-lofted clubs resemble a spoon or shovel and ever since we were infants we have been taught that spoons and shovels are for scooping. And most players are afraid that the longer, straighter-faced clubs won't get the ball up in the air, so again they scoop and try to lift it.

Assuming you don't flat-out top the ball, this scooping action at best creates a weak, ineffective ball flight in most cases. It's for this reason, in particular, that so many golfers feel they don't hit the ball far enough. The 7-iron might go sufficiently farther than the 8, but the 6 goes only a little farther than the 7, while the 3- and 4-irons don't go as far as the 5.

That's because in trying to get "under" the ball you add loft to the club. With short irons this effect is minimal because of the loft already built into the club. Adding four or five degrees of loft to a 50-degree pitching wedge is a change of only about 10 percent. However, adding the same amount of loft to a 24-degree 3-iron results in a difference of more than 20 percent.

37

So when the ball is on the ground, you must swing down to get proper contact and good results. With all but the most extreme low-profile clubs, the center of the club at address will be above the center of the ball. So to get center-to-center contact, the club must be moving downward as it approaches impact. Trust the loft of the club to get the ball airborne. It will work.

The same awareness of the relationship between the center of the ball and the center of the club dictates a swing shape that is at least level or, more accurately, slightly ascending through the ball with a driver. Simply stated, when the ball is teed up, swing up; if the ball isn't up, don't!

The correct angle of approach is a very important part of achieving compatability between direction and distance. With shorter irons like the 8, 9 or wedge, the club should be coming in on the steepest angle of approach. This will create more backspin and greater accuracy. As the clubs get longer, the angle of approach should start to become shallower. Part of this change is dictated by the differences in the clubs. The clubs with shorter shafts will have a shorter radius and, as a result, a slightly sharper angle of approach to the ball. However, too many golfers keep the same steep angle with the longer clubs. As the angle of approach needs to flatten out with the longer clubs, your swing path must change to accommodate this.

The single best example of how the angle of approach should change when more distance is needed, as well as how interrelated your swing path and angle of approach are, lies in watching all those field-goal kickers on the football field. Ever stop to wonder why there are hardly any more straight-on kickers in the National Football League? A few years ago, goalposts were moved from the goal line back ten yards to the end line. Immediately the distance difference created the need for change. Instead of wanting accurate short-distance kickers, the call went out for people who could strike from 45 to 55 yards away. Enter the "soccer-style" kicker. Instead of striking the ball with his foot traveling down the line of flight at a relatively steep angle of approach, the soccer-style kicker uses a swing path for his leg that is much more from inside the line of flight. The result is a shallower angle of approach of the foot and a more direct hit, resulting in much greater distance capability. No longer does the ball turn end over end as rapidly as it used to when the straight-on kicker produced a lot of backspin with his steeper attack angle. This change in style isn't without its negatives, though. The shallower attack angle brings with it a lower starting trajectory which causes both kicker and holder to eat a few footballs now and then.

The football analogy can help us to remember that the trajectory of our golf shots is greatly affected by the angle of approach of our swing. When wondering about the angle of ap-

As they kick, so shall ye swing

The path of the swing and angle of approach to the ball determines the flight of a place-kick in football just as it does a shot in golf. Here Ray Wersching, the soccer-style kicker for the Super Bowl champion San Francisco 49ers, swings the side of his foot into the ball on an inside-to-inside path and at a shallow angle. This is similar to the swing shape you want with a driver and the other longer clubs. It produces a lower trajectory and more distance. A straight-on kicker would swing his toe into the ball on a down-the-line path and at a steeper angle, getting a higher, straighter but shorter flight. This would be similar to a short-iron shot in golf, although you want even that short-iron swing to travel on a slightly inside-to-inside path. And although the shallower, more inside-to-inside path might not produce quite as accurate a shot (you don't need as much accuracy with the longer clubs anyway), it isn't bad, in either football or golf. This is one of four field goals Wersching kicked against Cincinnati in Super Bowl XVI to tie the record.

Ball on ground—swing down

If the ball is on the ground, the angle of approach should be downward to get the ball in the air.

Ball in air—swing up

If the ball is on a tee, the angle of approach should be at least level and preferably upward to achieve optimum trajectory. Note that the tee has been left untouched.

proach for any particular shot, all you have to do is remember the greater the distance needs, the shallower the angle, and the greater the directional needs, the steeper the angle.

Probably the most misunderstood error in the average golfer's game is the popped-up tee shot. It's the most misunderstood because of the way the golfer approaches the problem—if you'll pardon the pun. Most popped-up tee shots are immediately followed with, "Damn, I got under the ball again!" Wrong, wrong, wrong! The popped-up tee shot results from hitting DOWN on the ball too much, not from going under it. But the poor fellow who thinks otherwise starts to compound his problems. In trying to avoid swinging under the ball he hits down more on the ball, improving his swing to the point that the ball just misses his left shoulder and ear as it goes zipping by. If you have trouble with rainbow tee shots, try topping the ball for awhile. This should have the effect of making your swing shallower and giving you more solid contact. It also will help reduce the number of white marks on the top of your driver! Every so often I will get a student who wants to know which way the tee should fly after a perfect tee shot . . . backward or forward? The answer is—nowhere! Because they strike the ball on a slightly ascending path, the better players actually leave the tee in the ground more times than not.

5. POINT OF CONTACT
On-Center Hits Are the Ideal, Not the Reality

Have you noticed that when you're swinging well you seem to strike the ball with the sweet spot of the club every time, but when your swing is a little off, no shot feels solid? On-center hits and a good swing go hand-in-hand, as do on-center hits and consistent ball-flight patterns.

All impact factors are interrelated. But the point of contact between club and ball is totally dependent on the other factors. Thus, that point of contact becomes a valid indicator, not only of what you have done right but what you may have done wrong in your swing.

Ball-flight patterns are distorted by off-center hits. Shots struck on the toe will tend to start right and hook back to the left and shots hit on the heel will start left and slice right, especially with a wood, which has a curved face. So the normal path-face relationship is disrupted. On the other hand, solidly struck shots that fly errantly can be diagnosed as path or face problems with a great degree of accuracy.

With some knowledge and awareness, you also can use shots struck off-center to diagnose your swing problem. Shots struck high or low on the clubface, for example, generally can be attributed to an incorrect angle of approach. Too steep an angle usually causes the balls to be hit high on the face, while too shallow an approach most often results in contact low on the club.

Probably the most common mis-hit for the average golfer is toward the toe of the club, which is an indicator of the outside-in swing path you want to eliminate. Conversely, when the better player misses the sweet spot, it usually is toward the heel of the club because he is approaching the ball too much from the inside—but at least it is from the inside, the goal you should be seeking.

So, being aware of where the ball is struck on the face can help you correct errors in both your path and angle of attack. You must develop the sensitivity that gives you that awareness. If you can't distinguish the different points of contact on the clubface, your ability to consistently create on-center

Errant hits distort flight

Shots struck off-center will not fly normally according to the dictates of path and clubface position because the club twists and causes a "gear effect" that imparts spin on the ball. Shots hit on the toe will tend to start right and probably will hook left. Shots hit on the heel will tend to start left and slice right.

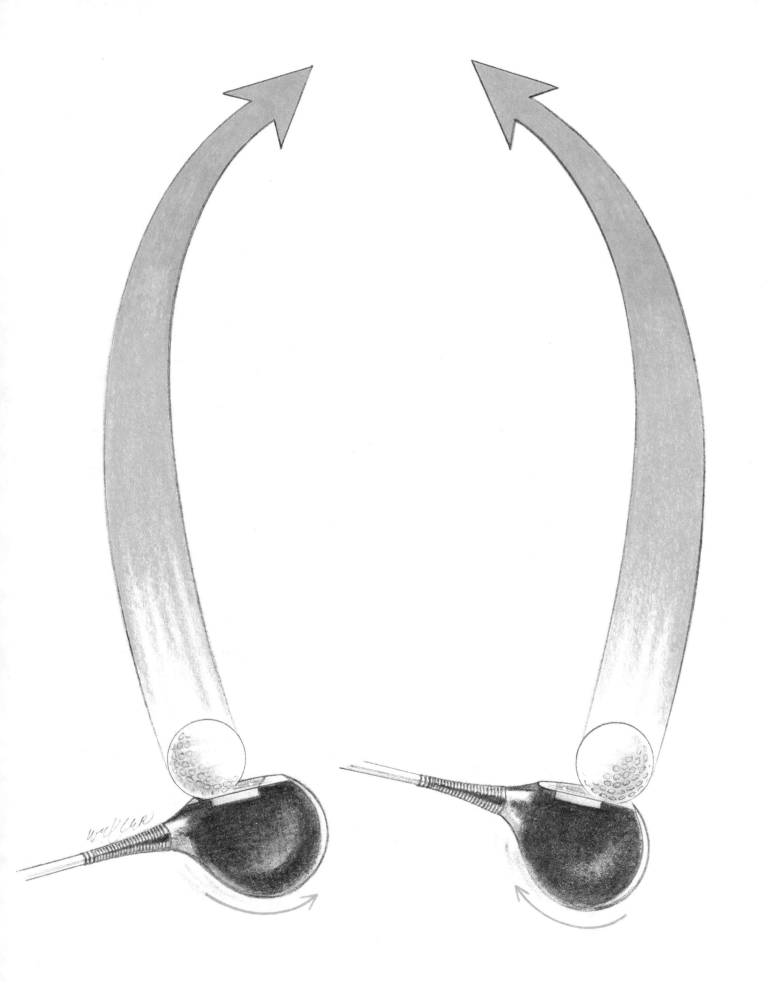

hits will be greatly diminished if not eliminated.

This sensitivity starts with your ability to feel the clubhead throughout the swing. Always in your swing development you should be able to feel where the clubhead is, because this is critical to distinguishing the point of contact and thus creating those on-center hits.

Golf is a bit of Catch-22 in that a good golf swing creates on-center hits, whereas on-center hits are needed to create a good golf swing. So where do we get on the merry-go-round?

It starts with the concept that solid contact is the first priority in your swing development. Let that solid contact govern your rate of progress. When and if you make a change in your swing, stay with it until solid shots become the rule rather than the exception. Only then should you proceed to your next stage of development.

So how are on-center hits accomplished? To begin with, consciously trying to strike the ball with the center of the clubface is folly. The clubhead is traveling 85-90 miles an hour or more at impact, certainly faster than the eye can see, so directly predetermining an on-center hit is unlikely.

What you can do is develop the correct swing path from the inside, marry it to the proper clubface position and angle of approach for the club you are using, then swing with a speed that allows the proper sequential movement of your swing. That may sound like a lot to do, but it really isn't that difficult if you concern yourself with it at the right time, and the right time is at the very beginning of your swing development.

Start by establishing solid contact with the putter on very short putts. Progress to longer and longer putts, trying for precise on-center contact, then to chip shots, pitch shots and finally full swings.

When your ability to make solid contact begins to erode, do the same things that athletes do in other sports. For example, a baseball hitter with the count 0-2 against him doesn't try to hit with power. He shortens his swing, reduces his hand pressure and tries to flick the bat at the ball to insure contact. A good boxer doesn't begin a fight swinging wildly, trying for a one-punch knockout. He starts with small punches, jabs and hooks to establish contact and find the range. A tennis player who misses on his first serve eases up on the second. He reduces his power and just tries to get the ball in play instead of blowing it past his opponent.

That philosophy also applies to golf. Ease up a little if you are mis-hitting shots. A three-quarter swing that produces solid contact is much more efficient than a full swing that doesn't.

In summary, you cannot play golf to your potential without being able to feel and create on-center hits, so everything you do with your swing should be based on how it affects that solid contact.

WHAT YOU NEED TO KNOW ABOUT THE LEARNING PROCESS

"TELL YOURSELF YOU'RE A HELL OF A WALKER."

Students often ask me if I think about certain actions in the golf swing while I am making shots on the course. My answer is that I don't think about swing particulars while I'm playing, but I certainly did while I was learning them.

To learn something, you must think about it consciously until you reach the point where you can do it subconsciously, trusting your body to perform the act without your mind interfering.

The length of time it takes to learn something new varies. The more complicated the undertaking, the longer you must allow. You can't possibly learn a golf swing in the same period of time it takes to refine one part of the swing.

Depending on how long and how regularly you work at it, developing a new muscle habit or motor skill usually takes from 21 to 35 days, studies show. But in replacing a part or all of your golf swing you will require more time than that, because you are trying to instill a new habit and eliminate an old one at the same time.

When we discuss how long it takes to develop a new habit, we have to look at the extent of development and how thoroughly the habit is ingrained. Developing the new pattern until you begin to see some success doesn't take all that long. Developing the new pattern until you don't have to think about it anymore and still have it happen regularly is quite another matter. That takes a lot of time.

For example, I don't have to think about my right foot action when I'm hitting balls on the practice tee. It works beautifully. I don't have to think about it when I play a casual round on the course. It works pretty well. But when I compete in a tournament, my tension level rises, my body gets more active, my legs start to move faster and faster and pretty soon I revert back to my old habit of moving my right foot and leg too quickly. So I might have to use a conscious thought in a tournament to maintain my right foot position through impact.

Unless a person was fortunate enough to begin as a youngster under proper tutelage and develop nothing but good habits (and I don't know many golfers like that), he will always, at some point in time, have to consciously think about overcoming bad habits. No matter how much he has worked on them, they occasionally will creep back in and must be overcome again. Each time this happens, however, it should be easier to make the correction.

When you are working on a change, you should be able to see some immediate improvement. We like to tell the participants in our Golf Digest Instructional Schools that they will hit enough good shots that particular week to know that what they are working on is effective. They also will hit enough bad shots to know that they don't have it licked. The same philosophy applies to you. The learning curve does not ascend in a straight line but has peaks and valleys along the way. Many persons trying to learn a golf swing never get themselves through the valleys. Every time the curve turns downward they begin looking for a new thought, not realizing that this may be only a brief downturn before they start upward again toward another plateau, a more advanced level of execution. If you

change your goals or your thought processes every time you have a bad practice session or a couple of bad rounds in a row, your learning curve probably will flatten out or even go downhill.

Many players I see not only don't keep a single train of thought for days or weeks, they don't even keep it from shot to shot. If they hit a bad shot in a practice session they ask, "What did I do wrong?" In the first place, you shouldn't be concerned with what you did wrong but rather what you didn't do right. And you shouldn't worry about one particular shot. There could be a hundred reasons why you struck it badly, and if you start to worry about it you will undermine your practice session. You must develop a pattern of shots before you can come to a conclusion. If you hit a dozen bad shots in a row, then it's realistic to expect that you have a problem. At that point you can sit down and try to work out a solution, but certainly not until then.

So you must set your goals and give yourself enough time to make a permanent improvement instead of pushing the panic button whenever things go a little wrong. Three to five weeks, if you work at it during that period, should be enough time for you to determine if you are making it. At that point you either have your concepts firmly implanted in your mind and are on the road to improvement physically or you have confused lack of execution with lack of understanding and are in a total mess. If the latter is the case, you have to go back, either to this book or to the instructor with whom you are working, and get straightened out.

When learning, you must put yourself in an ideal learning environment to give yourself the best possible chance for success. Go to a part of the practice tee that is removed from everybody else if possible. Learning is difficult and learning a motor skill is particularly difficult. A college student couldn't achieve the same success if he studied every night in the middle of a crowded student union as opposed to a quiet corner in the library, where he could concentrate. Similarly, you must eliminate as many distractions as possible when you practice.

There is a reason why Ben Hogan didn't want people watching him practice, why Lee Trevino often goes to another golf course to practice during a tournament. A better player likes to put himself in a position where he has no fear of embarrassment. When you learn, you are going to make mistakes, and you are going to learn from them. The better player doesn't want to make those mistakes in front of other people. His fear of failure supersedes his desire to change. Therefore he finds it difficult to work on his golf game.

That is true of all of us, probably to a greater extent than with the professionals. *We are more embarrassed by our failures than we are encouraged by our successes.* That's why you must put your-

self in a position where fear of failure is not a problem. Once you do that, you allow yourself both physically and mentally to work out some positive changes.

You should carefully monitor the length of your practice sessions. I'm convinced that you can train yourself to perform better with shorter and more frequent periods of practice than in long, backbreaking sessions. I would rather see you end your practice session too soon than carry it on too long. You should quit when you feel you could hit a few more shots. Leave the session on a high note. The problem is that most players wind up their practice sessions with the driver and as soon as they start hitting it well they want to keep hitting it better and better. Sooner or later mental and physical fatigue sets in, or they start pushing themselves so hard that physical tension creeps in. At that point, productivity vanishes.

I suggest setting a limit of 30 to 45 minutes for each practice session. You might be able to do that three or four times in the course of a day if you have the time, but not longer than that at any one stretch. Have your goals in mind before you begin, then monitor yourself closely. As soon as you begin to see a decline in productivity, when your shots start flying errantly, quit, even if you are 10 to 15 minutes short of your allotted time. To continue will only make things worse, not better, and you will undo the good you have accomplished.

As you ingest and digest the thoughts in this book, your attitude in perceiving yourself and your objectives can be helpful—or particularly harmful—to your learning cause.

For example, many persons are too hard on themselves. We are a power-oriented society, bound for success at all costs and quickly. Unfortunately, the qualities of aggressiveness, ambition and drive that often make individuals successful in life and in their jobs make them unsuccessful in golf. The game requires a certain amount of level-headedness, composure, patience and positive attitude that some persons don't have.

Consider, for example, a physician. I don't know if all the doctors in the world would agree with this, but I feel that most are trained to think from negative to positive. The first question a doctor asks when he sees you is, "What's wrong with you?" That's also usually the first question a doctor asks when I give one a lesson. As soon as he hits one bad shot he'll ask, "What did I do wrong?" He's used to getting the negative input so he can diagnose and eventually arrive at a positive aspect. But when he pursues golf with that kind of negative outlook, he inhibits the amount of progress he can make. Rather than worrying about what he is doing wrong, he should concentrate on what to do correctly and positively.

On the other hand, there *are* some positive lessons to be learned from one's attitude toward life, but again they escape too many would-be golf-ers. The basic lesson is that in golf, as in life, you don't get something for nothing. A man who thinks nothing of devoting 16 or 18 hours a day to make his business successful may spend his life looking for the secret in golf. There is none. I know of no way to train your body to perform the golf swing without paying the price in hours and sweat.

So make a realistic evaluation of what you are trying to accomplish in golf. That way you can have realistic expectations. *Talent, time* and *technique* are the three keys that determine how well you will ever play this game. The two variables you can do something about are technique, which this book or a competent instructor can provide, and time. I'll tell you how to devote time in the correct fashion to improve your technique, but only you can determine *how much* time you spend. You can't read this book or take a couple of lessons and expect the process to have sprinkled you with magic dust so you can go back to your job six days a week, play golf only on Sunday and be a scratch player.

Set your level of expectation based on your *talent* and how much *time* you plan to spend improving your *technique* . . . and be realistic about it. *Unrealistic expectations create unmanageable tension, which in turn creates uncontrollable physical actions* and impedes any progress you could hope to make.

To carry that point a step further, let me talk about *comfort zones* in regard to your golf score. This is simply the zone in which your subconscious self-image tells you your scores should fall. Your comfort zone can really be a "discomfort" zone if it is too low. If your self-image is that of a player who should shoot between 72 and 75 but realistically your physical ability dictates that you should shoot no better than 80, you're in trouble. You will put so much pressure and tension on yourself that you'll probably end up shooting 85.

On the other hand, the comfort zone or expectation level of many golfers is too high. You might have the ability to shoot between 72 and 76, but if your comfort zone is between 77 and 80, you'll find a way to get there. If your subconscious self-image is one of a 77-80 player, your creative subconscious, whose job it is to fulfill the self-image, will make sure that happens. You may shoot 36 or 37 on the front nine, but you'll come back in 42 or 41 every time.

What I'm getting at is *imagination* and using it to develop the self-image that, along with intelligent physical work, will make you a better player. *Unless the mind imagines, the body cannot perform.* No amount of willpower and perseverence will do you any good unless you couple it with the proper use of your imagination. You can hit balls every day until the moon comes up and your scores won't get any better if your self-image is that of a hacker.

To illustrate, if I were to ask you to walk the length of a 40-foot steel beam that is two feet wide, you would have

no trouble doing it when the beam is resting on the ground. If I were to elevate the beam two feet into the air, you still would have no problem. However, I suspect that if I raised that same beam 100 feet into the air, you would have a serious problem walking its length, because you would imagine you were going to kill yourself. You would look down at the ground and envision the red splotch there where your imagination would be telling you you were going to end up. And sure enough, you would. No matter how strong your will to walk the length of that beam, your imagination would knock you overboard within a few steps.

To be able to walk that beam 100 feet in the air you would have to improve your self-image. You would have to tell yourself that you're a hell of a walker, that you have always been able to walk in a two-foot area and there is no reason you can't do it now. Imagine yourself walking across the beam, convince your subconscious you can do this and you will.

That phenomenon applies to virtually every activity and especially to golf. So when you are learning and when you are playing, you had better imagine yourself being successful and accomplishing your objectives. If you have any doubts, you will fail. Your imagination will win over your willpower every time.

There is a corollary to that of which you also must be aware. The mind must imagine before the body can per-

51

form, but the *mind cannot imagine what the body cannot perform.* You may want to hit a gentle draw around a dogleg and might try your mightiest to visualize that kind of shot, but unless you are physically able to hit it and have done so before, your mental computer will short-circuit.

That's where your willpower comes in. You must work at developing your swing to the point where you have confidence in it for a long enough period of time so that it will work on the course without your having to think about it. You must organize your thoughts and come up with a list of swing keys, any one of which you might use on a particular day. Then go play, forget about your swing and let your imagination take over. Physical ability and imagination are both vital, but they must act in concert, not in conflict. When you reach the point in your development that you quit worrying about your swing during a bad round and start being concerned over why you can't perform that swing, you will have arrived as a *player.*

Which brings up my final point. This book is designed to help you improve your golf swing. Presumably, by improving your swing you are going to improve your ability to score, because you will hit more good shots. But you must not always make your swing the scapegoat. On the practice range you learn, but the ultimate execution of the golf swing occurs not there but on the golf course. And that, with its attendant concerns over score,

hazards and the like, is quite a different matter than executing the swing on the practice range.

Let's say you have three objectives—to change your hand action, to change your angle of approach and to improve your right foot action, for example. When attacking each of these objectives, keep in mind that you haven't accomplished any of them until you can execute them on the course. Too many players think they have accomplished an objective when they can perform it on the driving range. So they immediately jump to No. 2 and then to No. 3. All this time they haven't played a round of golf. When they finally do go to the course with the new parts of their swing well in hand, they find they haven't learned to execute and trust the correct hand action on the golf course, so that breaks down. This in turn causes breakdowns in the correct angle of approach and the right foot action. So they are suddenly right back where they started and think the whole process has been a waste of time.

In reality, you should pursue just one objective at a time, first learning to perform the correct action on the practice range and then learning to execute it on the course. Once you have done this, go back to the range and pursue objective No. 2 in the same manner.

The whole point of your effort in reading this book is not to make you a better practice range player but a better golf course player. To accomplish that, you must play on a course. There are two measuring sticks for success when you are trying to improve your swing. The first is when you begin to see improvement in your ball flight and your consistency on the practice range, which means the new part of your swing is starting to take shape. The second comes when you see the same thing on the golf course, which means you are learning to execute it under all the distractions and tensions you find out there.

So keep going to the course while you are learning. You will have more fun and you will find it a much sounder and quicker way to reap the rewards from all your hard work, the joy of continued improvement in your play.

CHAPTER · 4

THE INSIDE PATH PROGRAM

AN OVERVIEW

In this section I will take you through the four stages of development that can transform you from a beginner, or wherever you are in the spectrum at the moment, to an accomplished golfer.

You will learn first to produce speed in your swing. I'm convinced that all great players—Jack Nicklaus, Arnold Palmer and the like—created speed first when they were learning the game, then developed control of that speed. I will help you learn to develop quality speed, that produced by the correct muscles. Then I will tell you how to control that speed, how to control your swing path so that it comes from the inside and how to control the clubface so you can square it at impact.

We will start by simply learning to control your hands and arms in a small swing, controlling the swing path and the blade of your club so you can get the ball properly in the air and hit it straight, even if it goes only 10 yards.

Once your hand and arm control is developed, you will learn to incorporate that into a little bigger motion, still without calling the lower body into use actively. From there we will progress to a full range of motion with your hands and arms swinging and the body pivoting, but not with a full-speed motion. Your arms will swing fully, your body responding accordingly. Then you will learn to swing with full motion and full speed, active with both your upper body and lower body. Finally, you will learn to do this at your maximum controllable speed, as fast as you can while maintaining your ability to swing the club on the right path, square the blade properly and consistently make on-center hits.

Your hands unlock your upper body, so you must train your hands first, keeping your wrists flexible so the hands can move. Once your hand action is developed, you learn to move your hands and wrists with your arms,

STAGE I
MASTERING THE FIRST SWING: Swinging of the hands and clubhead from the arms

STAGE II
MASTERING THE SECOND SWING: Swinging the arms from the shoulders

STAGE III
MASTERING THE PIVOT of the body that supports the first and second swings

STAGE IV
MASTERING THE TIMING that will allow you to put it all together—swinging with the correct speed-producing muscles on the correct inside path

developing a full-arm swing and subsequently a correct shoulder action.

Similarly, your feet unlock your lower body. You have to learn good footwork before you can incorporate the correct action of the legs and hips into your swing.

Once you have learned the correct action of the upper and lower halves, you will be able to use them the way they are supposed to be used—the body allowing the arms to swing and the arms allowing the hands to hit.

One thing is certain. If a part of your body is not working correctly, you don't eliminate it as the cure. You teach it to work the right way. Golfers often have been taught not to use their hands, to be passive with them. That's because they were using their hands incorrectly. But that's not the answer. You must learn to create an active release of the hands through impact before you can have a passive release that results from the swinging of the arms.

Proper training of the shoulders also is often ignored. Your shoulders should be basically followers in the swing. To properly create an angle in the backswing, your hands must start the clubhead first, your arms pick up the rhythm of your hands to complete the flow of the backswing and the shoulders follow along. But often they do not. Often, usually because of tension, they resist or even lead. If this is true with you, then the first thing you must do is train your shoulders to turn properly. Once they are turning

properly and are occupying the correct space, then you can let them become passive and they will respond to your arm swing in that same correct fashion.

Golf is not a left-sided game, nor is it a right-sided game. Golf is a two-sided game. All the muscles in your body serve a purpose in the golf swing, at some point in time, so you must use them all correctly to reach your potential. Both sides must work harmoniously, which means you must train them both to move correctly.

The days of teaching left-side dominance in order to overcome the failings of the right side are over as far as I'm concerned. A few years ago my left side was a lot stronger than it is now. I could do 25 push-ups with the left arm alone. I could take a weighted training club and hold it at the top of the swing with my left hand alone and my arm wouldn't even quiver. I could hit a 4-wood 185 yards with my left arm alone. But when I put my right hand back on the club, my instinctive desire to use my right side incorrectly still overcame the left side. The right side, for right-handers, is in a position to dominate and overpower, and it wasn't until I started consciously training my right side to move correctly that I began to improve my golf swing. My left side has weakened, but my golf swing as a whole is a lot stronger than it ever was.

Ultimately, for the sake of consistency, you want your left side to pace and control your swing. But you must put your right side in position and train it to move correctly to allow the left side to do that. If left-side strength alone could accomplish it, you would see all the players on the professional tour with massive left arms. But their arms are proportional in size, which means the pros are using both sides of their bodies together.

Your objective in this development program will be first to train your speed muscles—those from your elbows to your fingertips—to work correctly, then to train the rest of your body to provide support so that eventually you can swing at maximum speed under control. Training the speed muscles means just that. It does not mean swinging at maximum speed, at least until you can do so under control. That won't happen until you are well into the fourth and final stage of your development.

Let me give you an analogy that illustrates why you should learn in this manner. Take a pen in hand and write your name very small. You do it solely with your fingers. Now write your name a bit larger, and you'll use your fingers and hand. Now write in very large letters and you'll find your fingers, hand and arm all come into play. If you write your name across a billboard, all parts of your body will be used. But the controlling factor is always in your fingers.

The same is true with your golf swing. No matter how long and powerful your swing gets, it always is controlled by your hands. To a degree, everything else becomes supportive.

When the speed and effort of the body becomes greater than the strength of the hands can handle, there will be a breakdown in your swing.

There is another important reason, often overlooked, for learning to control your swing correctly with your hands—the tension factor. There will always be a certain level of tension on the golf course, and that level will rise under the heat of competition or when you get into a tight situation. That's true for you, for me and for Jack Nicklaus. If your golf swing requires that your tension level be low before you can execute it, you're going to be in trouble when that level goes up.

For example, if the hinging of your hands and wrists is dependent on a light grip pressure that allows the weight of the clubhead to create the angle, what will happen when your grip pressure increases? The answer is simple—instead of having a two-lever swing under pressure, you will revert to more of a one-lever motion.

So you can't ignore tension, nor can you always eliminate it. You must learn to perform with it. If you sense tension and relate that to an inability to perform, your tension increases that much more. On the other hand, if you know you can perform under tension, if you know you can make a shot even if your life depends on it, your tension actually will be reduced.

CHAPTER · 5

PRELIMINARIES

GRIP AND PREPARATION

This swing-building program requires that you actually hit balls on a practice range in a methodical step-by-step manner. Before doing so, let's briefly discuss the preswing fundamentals of how you grip the club and how you set up to the ball.

GRIP

The grip creates the contact between you and the club. The grip can either promote or inhibit hand action. And that is how it should be approached, based strictly on your requirements.

Earlier on in golf, in the "classic" swing described previously, the hands and wrists had to supply a lot of the movement of the club and as a result the grip was more finger-oriented. It allowed for more wrist flexion to compensate for the reduced freedom of arm swing and also helped produce the desired right-to-left ball flight needed for sufficient distance.

The modern golf courses and players have precipitated a quite different grip to serve the needs of today. Emphasis on hand action to create clubhead motion is diminished. The greater allowance for free arm motion has led to a more palm-oriented positioning of the club in the hands, which also serves to produce higher, softer, ball flights that don't hook quite as much.

The ideal grip is not a palm grip. It is not a finger grip. It is a combination of the two, and the correct combination for you depends on what you will be trying to achieve with your swing.

The positioning of the hands, whether left, neutral, or right on the grip, should be dictated by your needs in returning the clubface to the desired impact position. If you have trouble hooking the ball too often, then a more leftward grip will be helpful. Probably the bigger problem is that of not being able to eliminate a slice. The more difficult it is for you to produce a right-to-left ball flight, the more your hands should be turned to the right of center. The key here is that the more you hold the club in the fingers, especially the fingers of the left hand, the more flexibility you have in the wrist joints and the more hand action is allowed. The more the grip is in the palm, the more your flexibility is restricted and the less hand action you can generate.

To assume the left-hand grip, set the club in position and place your open hand against the side of the handle so the handle lies at an angle running from the middle joint of the forefinger across the knuckle joint of the little finger and into the palm. The butt end of the club should lie just below the heel pad. Now close your hand over the club, placing your thumb slightly to the right of shaft center as you look at it. Make sure the club remains tucked underneath the heel pad and doesn't slip into the valley between the heel and thumb pads. At this point you should be able to hold the club aloft supported only by the forefinger and in the heel pad.

How you adjust this combination to best suit your purposes will depend on whether you need more or less hand action in your swing. Since most players need more flexibility in the hands and wrist joints, they should set the club more toward the fingers, or deeper underneath the heel pad. If you feel you are too "handsy" and need more stability, the club should be angled

higher into the palm. But never let the butt end slip over the muscle of the heel pad. Always keep it under, so the pad keeps pressure downward on the handle while the fingers create pressure upward.

To check your palm-finger ratio, stand sideways to a mirror and assume your grip and address position, bending from the hips and letting your arms hang. Note that when the club is properly soled on the floor the shaft sits at an angle to your forearm. The greater that angle, the more the club is in the fingers of your left hand. The smaller the angle, the more it is up in the palm.

Note also that the more the club is in the fingers, the more your left hand will tend to turn to the right, placed more over the top of the club. The more it is in the palm, the more it will be in a straight or "neutral" position.

The right-hand grip is tremendously important, especially for the majority of players who cannot generate enough hand speed. It is strictly with the fingers, never the palm. This gives you more flexibility with the right hand and wrist joint and allows more hand speed in the swing.

The analogy here is the baseball pitcher who grips the ball more with the tips of his fingers to throw a fastball and moves it back toward his palm to throw the change-up. He makes the same motion, but because he has reduced his wrist action with the grip change, the ball travels more slowly.

To place your right hand correctly, set the portions of your middle and

The three basic grip forms

The three basic grip forms are the overlap (A), in which the little finger of the right hand is overlapped over the forefinger of the left; the interlock (B), in which the little finger of the right hand and the forefinger of the left are interlocked; and the 10-finger (C), in which all the fingers are placed directly on the club. The overlap is considered the standard grip for players with normal or out-sized hands who have no problem with flexion at the wrist. Players with shorter fingers or thicker hands might benefit from the interlock grip. Those with smaller and weaker hands, or those who are having trouble releasing or turning over the club, should favor the 10-finger arrangement.

Note: A special short-shafted club is used in these photos to demonstrate the relationship between grip and clubface.

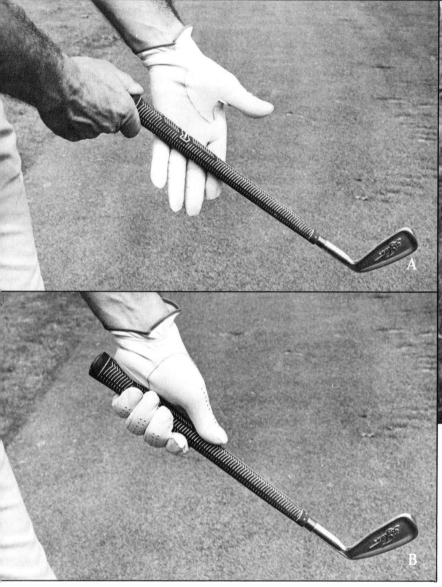

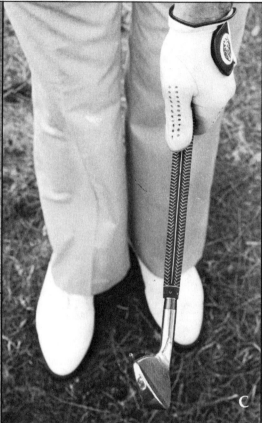

How to build left-hand grip

Assume the left-hand grip by placing the handle at the base of the palm as shown (A), making sure the heel pad is above the top of the handle. Close the fingers up to the palm (B) so you can feel pressure *down* on the handle with the heel pad and *up* from the bottom with the fingers, especially the last three fingers. From the front (C), the thumb should be slightly to the right of center.

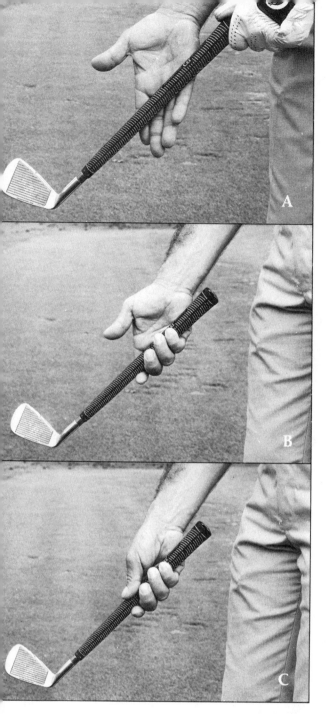

How to build right-hand grip

In assuming the right-hand grip, follow the same procedure you did in putting your left hand on the club, except that the handle lies more in the fingers. Angle it from a point between the second and third joints of the forefinger to a point under the heel pad as shown (A). When closed, the fingers—especially the forefinger—present a triggered appearance (B). This appearance is accentuated when the thumb is closed on the top of the handle, slightly to the left of center (C). Take care that the right-hand grip is more with the fingers, not too far into the palm. The pressure should be primarily with the last three fingers and only lightly with the thumb and forefinger.

The completed grip: palms facing

This is the completed *neutral* grip, the palms of both hands basically square to the clubface. The grip can be turned more to the right (as you look at it) to promote more hooking action or more to the left to prevent excessive hooking. Take care that in any position the palms basically face each other.

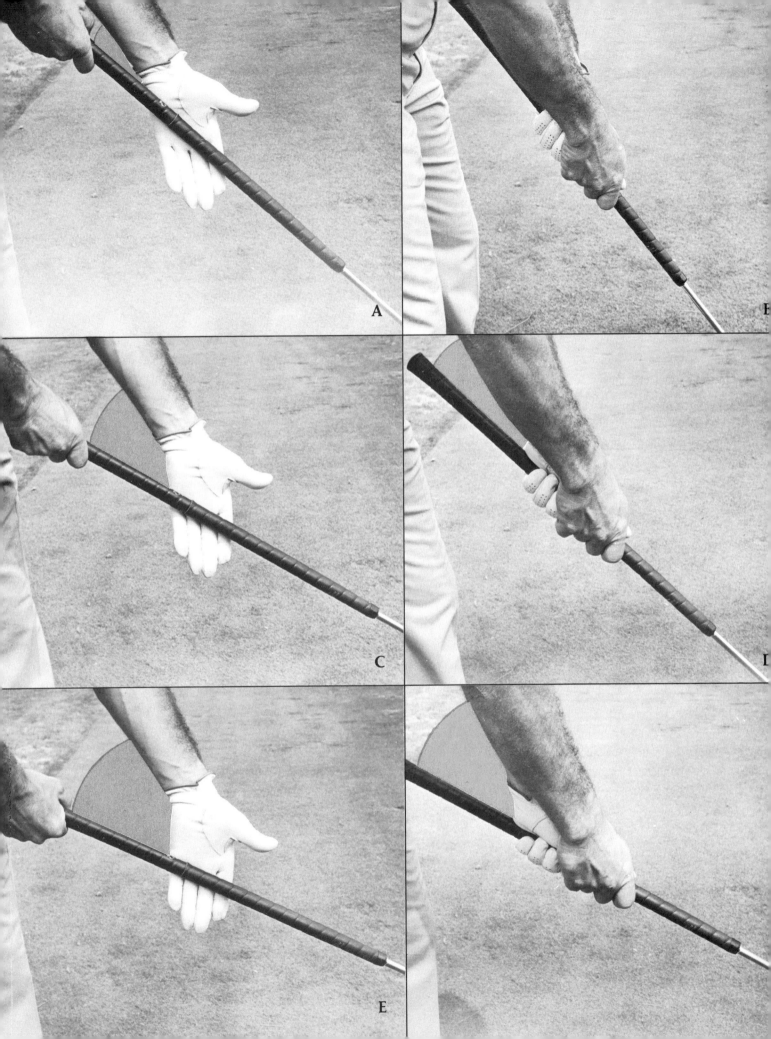

A

B

C

D

E

Your left-hand grip position determines your wrist flexion

The positioning of the handle in the left hand regulates the amount of flexion at the wrist in your swing. The special extended club handle used here helps to demonstrate this fact. If you grip the club more in the palm, angled higher toward the top of the heel pad (A), it creates a smaller shaft/arm angle (B) and inhibits hand and wrist action. A combination finger and palm grip (C) gives you a normal shaft/arm angle at address (D) and normal hand-wrist flexion. A grip more in the fingers (E) results in a greater shaft/arm angle (F) and promotes more hand and wrist action throughout the swing. You should diagnose your needs before determining which grip position you should adopt.

ring fingers that lie between the first and second joints underneath the club. Then close your hand so the area between the two pads butts snugly against the left thumb. Close your forefinger on the club, positioning it in the same manner you did the two middle fingers. It should have a slightly "triggered" appearance. Place your right thumb on the handle so the thumb pad rests to the left side. The area of the thumb from the joint down should be resting against the fleshy part of the palm at that point, forming a closed V. If the V is open, the thumb is too far down the side of the handle.

The little finger should overlap the forefinger of the left hand. Some players prefer that it rest in the crevice between the forefinger and middle finger of the left—I call this the "overlock" grip—on the premise that it better uni-

fies the two hands. The true overlap allows them more freedom in the right hand to rotate and turn the clubhead over. This is why the so-called ten-finger grip, in which the little finger of the right hand is actually placed on the club, can be effective for a player who has trouble creating rotation and hand speed.

The precise positioning of both hands on the club depends, of course, on the size of your hands, length of fingers and other variables. You probably will have to experiment and adjust a bit. But, within the context of what you are trying to do with your swing, the grip model described and illustrated is the one from which you should start.

Pressure in the grip is applied primarily with the last three fingers of each hand. Too much has been written and said about maintaining pressure in the last three fingers of the left and the middle two fingers of the right without mentioning the little finger of the right hand. It helps keep the hands together during the swing. You must have some pressure in the little finger of the right hand to help keep the valley of the right hand—that area between the pads—snug against the left thumb.

There should be no conscious pressure in the right thumb and forefinger. As you swing forward you will feel pressure against the thumb and forefinger, but that is *reactive* pressure, helping you to contain the angle I mentioned earlier. It is not active pressure.

Now, how much pressure? A firm grip as a result of swing speed is fine, but a firm grip to create swing speed is destructive. To explain that, let's start with the premise that, for most golfers, the pressure in the fingers at address should be enough just to hold the club off the ground. When the club is not in motion, it doesn't require a lot of pressure to hold it. As you start moving the club, the pressure in your fingers will increase in reaction to the speed of the club's movement. But if you prematurely increase the pressure in your hands, you will inhibit your ability to create movement and speed, because you will tighten the muscles in your hands and arms that produce that speed.

Now, while that change in pressure during the swing is going to occur, ideally it should be kept to a mini-mum, the grip pressure staying as constant as possible throughout. So your grip pressure at address should be representative of the pressure required during the swing, based on the swing you are going to generate. If you are capable of generating great clubhead speed, a considerable amount of pressure will be required to hold onto the club during the swing. If you start off with an exhorbitantly light grip pressure, you are going to have tremendous changes in the pressure from beginning to end of the swing. That creates a jerky movement and can be disastrous.

That's why a good player like Tom Watson, who generates great speed in his swing, feels like he holds the club firmly. He already has great speed, knows the feel of it and instinctively grips firmly enough to accommodate it so he keeps his pressure as constant as possible throughout the swing. But when a poorer player who has never felt hand and arm and clubhead speed starts off with a firm grip, he strangles his movement.

When I speak of firmness, I mean firmness in the fingers while keeping the wrist and forearm areas as relaxed as possible. Too many amateurs have relaxed fingers and tight wrists and arms, so instead of getting a wrist cock they get a finger cock. They let go of the club during the swing, with predictably unfortunate results.

So keep the forearms relaxed and grip as firmly as you think you need with the fingers. In the beginning, if you are working to develop swing speed, this should be just firmly enough to hold the club off the ground. As you begin to create more swing speed, you can hold the club commensurately firmer at address, but never so tightly that you inhibit the free movement of your hands and arms.

PREPARATION

It's amazing to me how many golfers make their swing the scapegoat for any and all errant shots. The fact is that most bad shots are predetermined by a preswing error—either in posture, aim, alignment or ball position.

Golf is one of those situations where two wrongs can make a right. The only problem lies in making all mistakes at the right time so they cancel out and produce a shot to target.

For that reason it is very important to make sure your preswing positions are compatible with your inswing desires. Just as your grip should fit your swing needs, your posture, ball position, aim and alignment should match your intended arm swing.

Your posture position largely determines the balance and shape of your golf swing. Unfortunately, for too many golfers some bad information has led to equally bad posture. Keys such as "sit down to the ball like a barstool " or "balance on your heels" or "keep your left arm straight" have created some memorable problems.

"Sitting down" to the ball at address puts your back too vertical and gives you too much knee flex. It puts your body in the way of your arm swing. If you have too much knee flex at address and maintain it during your backswing, chances are you are going to lose it in your forward swing. This means your lower body will be moving upward while you are trying to swing the club down and forward. The result will be that the momentum of your body will interfere with, instead of complement, the motion of your arm swing. Your golf swing will become a big isometric exercise, with parts of the body working in opposition to other parts. When this happens, you will exert a lot of effort without creating very much motion.

Balancing on your heels doesn't make any sense. How many sports can you think of that are played on the heels? When you make your backswing, your arms start from in front of you and go behind you, which transfers your weight toward your heels. So if you start on your heels, you will either fall backward or be forced to use a less-than-full backswing or swing the club up too vertically to maintain your balance. This is why some players swing the club so high on a too-upright plane. They know instinctively that if they get their arms behind them, they will fall over backward. It also creates short swings in order to maintain that same degree of balance.

The thought of keeping the left arm straight at address usually translates into a rigid left arm, which stiffens the entire upper body and creates a ten-

Your posture shapes your swing

Your posture should prepare your body for the type of swing you will be making. For the normal full iron shot (A), your weight should be evenly distributed or *slightly* favoring your right leg at address to predicate a more descending blow. With the longer clubs, especially the driver (B), feel that your right side is set more "under" your left side, with 55-60 percent of your weight favoring the right leg. This allows for a more ascending sweep through the ball.

Good posture promotes a balanced, free arm swing

Good posture determines the position that allows a free arm swing as well as good balance favoring the balls of the feet, the knees slightly flexed. As the club gets longer, the arms should be more extended from the body at address, as in the case of the pitching wedge (A), 5-iron (B), and driver (C).

sion that prevents you from swinging effectively. You get your arms locked to your shoulders.

Good posture is simply that which allows you to make an effective swing. Your upper body should be in a position to allow complete freedom of hand and arm motion. Your lower body should be in a position to move so it can support and complement the motion of your upper body. Good posture allows freedom of movement and creates proper balance.

To assume correct posture at address, balance your weight toward the balls of your feet. Your weight should be distributed fairly evenly for the short irons, progressively more to the right for each longer club. With the driver, when the ball is on a peg, your weight should be 55-60 percent on your right side. Your feet should be spread wide enough to keep you in balance for the particular swing you are making but not so wide as to lock your hips and legs. Experiment to find your best stance width for each club.

Flex your knees slightly, just enough to unlock them, and bend forward from the hips. Your arms should hang in a relaxed fashion, slightly extended, which allows them to swing free of the body and gives them room to return to the ball on an inside path. Avoid creating too vertical an arm hang which will make it difficult to swing your arms properly. Keep your back fairly straight and your shoulders relaxed. Your head should not droop—let the neck maintain approx-

imately a straight-line relationship with the rest of the spine.

How much your upper body is angled from the hips and how much your arms are extended will depend on the club in your hand. As we will discuss later, your swing shape varies from more upright with the shorter clubs to flatter with the longer ones. The flatter or more around your body the swing gets, the more your arms must be extended to accommodate that shape.

After your arms and body are prepared to perform properly, you need to be concerned with the positions of the golf ball, clubface and shaft. In fact, most good players use the correct positioning of the ball and club as the foundation from which they prepare their posture and body alignment.

I'd estimate that 90 percent of the golfers in the world play the ball too far forward in their stance. This creates excessive rotary action in the forward swing and makes them come at the ball from the outside. The left-heel position may be fine for a tour player with a strong lateral leg-drive—although I notice even most of the professionals play it farther back than they say they do. For most amateurs to play the ball off the left heel is inviting disaster. You are making your swing chase after the ball instead of bringing the ball back to your swing. Also there is a great misinterpretation in positioning the ball relative to the left heel. Since you generally cannot see the left heel at address many players think *left*

Play ball back in stance for shorter shots

The shorter the shot and the shorter the club in your hand, the farther back in your stance the ball should be played. But note that the ball position in relation to the left heel remains constant while the stance is narrowed—the right foot moved closer to the target—as the shot gets shorter. This moves your swing center closer to the target and closer to the ball, which in effect is moving the ball back.

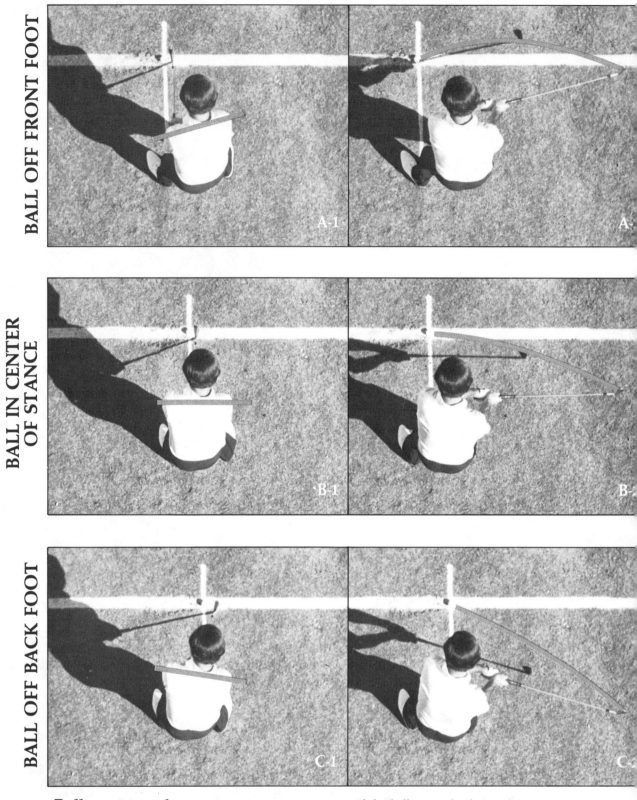

A-1

A-

B-1

B-

C-1

C-

Ball position determines swing path

Under normal conditions, the point at which you position the ball in your stance influences your shoulder alignment at address and the subsequent path of your swing. If the ball is too far forward (A), your shoulders will be set open or too far to the left, your swing path will be more to the outside going back, more from the outside coming forward and the ball will start to the left. With the ball properly positioned (B), your shoulders will be square and you will

be set up for the correct inside-to-inside swing path that starts the ball straight down your target line. If the ball is back in your stance (C), your shoulders will tend to close and you will swing on a more inside-to-outside path that will start the ball to the right.

75

Right knee must move to ball at impact

Your ball position for various clubs and shots should be adjusted so that the right knee can move laterally to a point even with the ball at impact. If the right knee cannot reach the ball, poor contact almost always will result.

heel but inadvertently position the ball relative to the *left toe*, which puts the ball even more forward.

The earlier classical players let the ball position range from nearer the right foot with the pitching wedge to as far forward as the left toe with the driver. This was done to accommodate poorer lies, the flex of the shafts and the torque or twisting characteristics of the clubs as well. Only recently have top players generally preferred a static ball position just off the left heel. This is a favored position to create a more lateral motion of the swing through the impact area. A forward ball position for the better player to aid in keeping the club on line longer is fine. But a forward ball position for the poorer player that causes an outward reaching and looping of the downswing is deadly.

I can give you no specific spot on which to position the ball. My recommendation is to put the ball far enough to the right in your stance so you can strike it from the inside. That may be a couple of inches or so inside the left heel with the driver and even farther to the right with the irons. When you position the ball so far to the right that your swing starts the ball too much to the right and requires excessive curvature to bring it back to the target, then you can start to move it forward slightly. Basically, the ball should be positioned just back of the point in your swing circle where you would start hitting it from the outside.

How you aim your clubface and

subsequently align your body has a great effect on your swing path, because you will instinctively react and try to return the face to a square position at impact. For example, if you are a slicer and close your clubface—aim it more to the left—to cure that slice, you will tend to get your right side set outside your left side and probably position the ball too far forward in your stance. This will further promote the outside-to-inside swing path that is undoubtedly causing your slice in the first place, and you will react to that by opening the blade in the impact area. This simply exaggerates your slice. If you hook the ball too much, opening the clubface—aiming it to the right—will cause you to swing back too much to the inside and probably too much to the outside on the forward swing. At the same time, your instincts will be to close the face or turn it over, further exaggerating your hook.

So your clubface should be aimed to promote the curvature of the ball you are trying to achieve. Basically, it should be set square or perpendicular to the line on which you want your ball to start. Since I am trying to get you to learn to hook the ball, if you are going to err in either direction, it should be toward a slightly open clubface rather than one that is closed.

Once your clubface is aimed, the parts of your body ideally should be aligned squarely. Eyes, shoulders, hips, knees and feet all should be aligned parallel with the line to your target.

If you can start from this square address position and return the club back to the ball from the inside, then go to it. However, if you have a lot of trouble swinging into the ball on an inside path, you may have to adjust by setting more to the right in relation to the target line. I'll discuss this more fully in Chapter 7.

If these preparatory concepts are now clear in your mind, you are ready to begin your developmental work.

CHAPTER · 6

THE INSIDE PATH PROGRAM

STAGE I: MASTERING THE FIRST SWING

...THE SWINGING OF THE HANDS AND CLUBHEAD FROM THE ARMS

WHAT TO DO

Place a ball on a tee and hit it 15 or 20 feet with a pitching wedge, feeling only your hands with virtually no arm swing. Once you have mastered this, do the same with a 6-iron, then a 3-iron and finally a 4- or 5-wood.

HOW TO DO IT

This is the first swing, the swinging of the clubhead with the hands and it is accomplished by a simple hinging and rehinging at the wrists. Stand to the ball with your feet together and keep your body quiet. Using only your hands and wrists, flick the ball off the tee and down the fairway. Your hands should form a 90-degree angle with your arms on both sides of the ball. The clubshaft should be approximately parallel to the ground and parallel to your target line both on the backswing and follow-through, the toe of the club pointing straight up in both positions.

At this point, you are simply using your hands to square the clubface through impact, although it is obvious that the action of the hands is creating some rotation of the arms. Let this rotation happen, neither trying to resist it nor trying purposely to create it. Don't be afraid to let the clubhead pass your hands after impact. Your left wrist will cup slightly on the follow-through, but that's fine. Eventually you will square the clubface with a more active rotation of your arms, but forearm rotation without good hand action is of little value, so first things first.

There is a crossover point in every swing when the clubhead passes the hands. In a full swing that crossover usually occurs at some point after impact. While learning the first swing, however, I want you to try to make that crossover exactly at the point of impact. Try to get the most movement of the clubhead with the least movement of the handle or grip end.

Stage I: The first swing of hands and clubhead

In building the first swing, the swinging of the hands and clubhead from the arms, try to develop as much clubhead movement as possible with the least amount of movement of the butt end of the club (A and B). Even though your primary concern is that the hands hinge from the wrists, there will be reactionary movement of the arms and body, especially with a wood club (C and D).

One big problem many golfers have with this exercise is that they confuse "over" with "around." Instead of simply letting the clubface turn over through impact, they swing the clubhead too much around to the left on the follow-through in an attempt to make that happen, usually because they relate clubhead rotation with body rotation. As a result, the clubhead goes too much around the body and not enough upward after impact.

So just hinge, unhinge and rehinge. Too much has been said and written about setting, retaining and releasing the angle through impact, and not enough emphasis has been placed on re-forming the angle after impact. In pursuing the goals of "extension" and "high follow-through" that they have been told is so important, too many golfers fail to rehinge or re-form the angle and so cost themselves a lot of clubhead speed.

Perform this little swing in a relaxed manner. Do not pursue distance. When you see the ball going farther than your effort would seem to dictate, you will know you are doing it correctly.

When you move into the longer clubs, the 6-iron, 3-iron and 4- or

Cross over at impact

Here a golf ball is stuck onto the end of the grip to help illustrate the crossover point in the swing. Note how the ball disappears behind the hands at impact, then reappears after impact. This shows that the clubhead has swung past the hands through the impact area.

Hinge and rehinge inward, not around

Hinge the club back, up and inward, then unhinge and rehinge it forward, up and inward. Don't let the club swing prematurely around your body during the follow-through in an attempt to square the clubface.

5-wood, you instinctively will use your arms more. Don't worry about it, but still try to feel the motion is made primarily with your hands.

Your ball flight at this point should be straight and relatively low, simply because you are not generating enough clubhead speed to get the ball high in the air, or enough spin to curve the ball.

WHAT YOU LEARN

The first swing lays the foundation for the ideal inside-to-inside swing path. It is virtually impossible to swing otherwise if you simply hinge, un-hinge and rehinge your hands to strike the ball.

Working with this swing will determine the level of your hand-eye coordination and how much effort you need to make in this area. If you can't strike the ball squarely with your hands in this small swing, you can't hope to use your hands correctly and consistently in the full swing. If this is the case with you, spending time with the first swing will develop your hand-eye coordination. You will train the muscles in your hands and wrists to move correctly, starting the clubhead away from the ball first and accelerating it through impact at what eventually will be your maximum potential speed. You also will learn the movement that ultimately will trigger your golf swing—the waggle. The hinging and unhinging of the hands here will be the key to starting your full swing correctly, a subject I'll discuss more thoroughly in Stage III.

Finally, working with this small swing will build consistency, feel and rhythm into your bigger swing. It will give you a taste, however small, of success in striking the golf ball properly, and success is perhaps the greatest motivator of all.

Left-hand-only drill

From a relatively narrow stance, with the ball on a tee, grip down a little on the club with your left hand only, the pressure in the last three fingers. Then simply cock your hand and clip the ball off the tee. Just hinge, unhinge and rehinge after impact. Form an angle on the backswing and tap down on the ball. Initially, the swing is with your left *hand* only. You may hold your left forearm with your right arm to keep it steady if you wish. When you begin to make consistent contact, gradually lower the ball until it is on the ground. This drill develops skill and strength in your left hand.

Right-hand-only drill

This is the·reverse of the left-hand-only drill. Grip down on the club with your right hand only, making sure your grip is in the proper position with the pressure in the last three fingers. Then just cock the hand and clip the ball off a tee as you did with the left—hinge, unhinge and rehinge. You may hold your right arm with your left to keep it steady if you wish. Again, as you gain proficiency, gradually lower the tee until the ball is on the ground.

THE INSIDE PATH PROGRAM

STAGE II: MASTERING THE SECOND SWING

...THE SWINGING OF THE ARMS FROM THE SHOULDERS

WHAT TO DO

In this stage you create the proper swing plane of the clubshaft and arms. You also create the descending blow in your swing.

Start your swing exactly as you did in Stage I, but now let your arms start to swing more, increasing the arm swing gradually until your hands are chest high on both the backswing and follow-through. Leave the ball on a tee until you feel your hands working fully, freely and correctly through the shot. Then gradually lower the tee and finally put the ball on the ground. Again start with a pitching wedge, progressing to a 6-iron, 3-iron and 4- or 5-wood.

HOW TO DO IT

In this stage you begin to learn the second swing, that of the arms swinging from the shoulders and transporting the hands and club.

At the beginning of this stage you still will be standing with your feet together, basically flat-footed. There will be no active movement of your body, although the shoulders and hips should turn in reaction to the swinging motion.

You still will set the angle immediately with your hands, starting the clubhead first away from the ball on the backswing. Your sensation still will be to hinge, unhinge and rehinge as you swing through impact. Your hands are controlling the movement. But now the swinging of your arms will make it feel as if the angle were being set a bit later in your backswing. That actually will happen, but that should not be your controlling thought. You still should feel as if there are two parts to your swing— your hands setting and your arms swinging. Later, in Stage III, we will blend those parts more into a whole.

Again, relax and feel the correct muscles creating speed in your swing.

Stage II: Make a fuller motion

In Stage II, the arms should swing the hands through a fuller range of motion. To allow this longer swing, let your body and legs respond passively to the swinging motion.

Never replace technique with effort, because excessive effort will prevent learning the correct technique. Let distance be the result of that technique. You'll find that even with this relatively small swing your clubhead speed will be much faster than you would have imagined.

At this point, once your arms are involved, you begin to be more concerned with forearm rotation, but only to the extent that you *let* your arms rotate with your hands and the clubface. Don't resist rotating the arms. As the club wants to rotate over, let the arms go with it. Feel like your left forearm and the back of your left hand become a unit. Your hands create the angle by hinging at the wrists while the forearms—particularly the left forearm—provide rotation to that angle. But at this point, remember, you are just letting that rotation of your arms happen naturally as you

87

Your swing has more width than you feel

To prove that your swing has plenty of width and you are really not picking up the club too quickly when you start with your hands, place a ball about 12 inches behind your play ball and, with a short iron, hinge the club back with your hands. You'll clip the back ball, which means the clubhead is not being picked up prematurely.

swing back and through. It is here that the proper plane of the swing is established. In Stage I the clubhead was moved on an extremely vertical plane. Now, because you have added the arm swing, the plane will flatten slightly. Your checkpoint to determine if your club is on plane will be to insure that the butt end of the club points directly at the ball in the initial stages of the backswing and then along the target line as you swing farther back.

Because you are using your hands so early and so actively, your swing will feel more vertical or more "up and down" than perhaps you are used to. Don't worry about that. For those of you who have been taught "extension" all your golfing lives, your swing still has plenty of width. If you don't believe that, if you feel you are picking the club up quickly on the takeaway, try a test for me. Place a ball 12 inches back of your play ball, set up with a pitching wedge and take the club back with your hands only. Despite the sensation of picking up the club, you'll find you clip the back ball on your takeaway. If you swing your arms as you set the angle with your hands, especially with the longer clubs, you'll clip a ball set back 18 inches or so. Since the top of that ball is only a little more than an inch and a half above the surface of the ground, you are really taking the club back a lot lower than you think.

Once you get the arms swinging in conjunction with the hand movement,

of course, you create two possibilities for getting your forward swing onto that dreaded outside path. The first is by a premature rotation of your body. Even though your body is supposed to be passive at this stage, your instincts to create speed with the bigger muscles may cause it to rotate and swing the arms, hands and club to the outside at the start of the forward swing. The second way to get on the outside path is to prematurely uncock the hands starting down, causing you to slap the club down from the outside.

As your swing gets longer, these tendencies will become even more pronounced, so guard against them now in this early stage of development. Cultivate the sensation of your arms letting the club move inward and downward from the top of your swing while your hands keep the angle set. Let your body remain quiet while the arms swing the club into the ball from the inside. Then your hands will unhinge and rehinge to produce the clubhead speed that gives you so much distance with so little effort. *The correct sequence of motion is hands-arms on the backswing, arms-hands on the forward swing.*

As soon as your hands and arms are swinging fully and freely together with all of the four clubs used in this stage, gradually lower the tee and continue to hit shots until you can do so successfully with the ball on the ground.

Now is the time to work on striking the ball with the correct descending blow that we discussed in Chapter 2.

"Pray" to feel arm rotation

If your level of arm tension allows you a free swing, as you hinge, unhinge and rehinge the club you will feel a rotation of the arms. Emulate this "prayer drill" without a club and feel the left arm rotate over the right in the backswing, the right arm rotate over the left in the follow-through.

Learn to take a divot in front, on the target side, of the ball. Drive the back of the ball down so you spin the front of the ball up.

At this point, ball position also comes into play. Play the ball opposite your right toe—remember, your feet are still close together—which will force you to strike down with a more descending blow. It also further insures that you strike the ball from the inside.

Here is where you begin to learn the critical shot in your development process—the low right-to-left shot, or draw. If you cannot hit the low draw, you cannot play golf to your potential. So now your shots must start to the right of your target and move back to the left. I don't really care, for the moment, if they start way right and hook way left, but you must establish that right-to-left pattern.

This is done through a combination of swinging on the inside path and rotating the clubface through impact. When you put the ball back—to the right—at address, this automatically will open your clubface or aim it more to the right at address. Obviously, if you are swinging from inside to outside the target line through impact with an open clubface, the shot will start to the right and keep going more that way. So now you must accentuate the rotation of your forearms and hands—not your shoulders—to square the clubface and produce that right-to-left action. This rotation need not be pronounced until you move into Stage III, but for the moment, you must be aware that the combination of swinging down from the inside and rotating gives you the desired right-to-left ball flight.

Continue to emphasize your hand action and a relaxed swing. Hinge, unhinge and rehinge, the only difference being that your increased rotation will eliminate some of the cupping through impact that you felt earlier.

Stay with this stage until you can consistently hit solid shots and control the ball flight with all the clubs—pitching wedge, 6-iron, 3-iron and 4-wood. Then you can advance to Stage III.

WHAT YOU LEARN

This stage provides a good test for a player at any level, beginner or low-handicapper, to determine if he or she is casting the club from the top or swinging down from the outside. If you can swing the club down from the inside, start the ball to the right and turn it back to the left, you are ready to move on to more advanced stages.

In Stage II you begin learning to build a small swing into a fuller motion. The bigger swing feels the same as the smaller one except for its size. You should devote the same percentage of time going through the various positions in your smallest swing and your biggest swing. In other words, if you spend 35 percent of your time changing directions in your full swing, you should spend 35 percent changing directions in the mini-swing. The elapsed time might differ, but the percentages should be the same. That's the way you teach yourself to time your golf swing consistently. I find it helpful, especially when I'm not playing much, to make a couple of partial swings before I hit a shot, concentrating on the same pace and timing I want to use in the full swing.

The same exercise will help you. For example, when you make a small swing, pay attention to how long your shoulders feel they stay turned during the change of directions at the top. If they don't feel they stay turned that long in your full swing, your timing is being thrown off by your shoulders.

Timing, of course, concerns not only the amount or percentage of time you spend doing things in your swing but also the *sequence* in which you do them. It's important to understand that you can have all the parts working but in the wrong sequence, causing you to mis-hit the shot. Also, if you don't have the right sequence, it is difficult if not impossible to spend the proper amount of time in the various stages of your swing. In Stage II, then, you should concentrate on a *hands-arms going back, arms-hands coming forward* sequence.

This also is the stage in which you begin to realize that every part of the body must contribute 100 percent of its fair share during the swing. If it does not, another part will take over, usually with unfortunate results. For example, if you have only 20 percent of the hand action you need to create the speed you want, that means 80

percent is missing. So your arms may assume half that burden and your shoulders the other half, which means you now are swinging with 20 percent of your necessary hand action, 140 percent of the correct arm action and 140 percent of the needed shoulder action.

Your solution to that problem is not to try to calm the shoulders or slow down the arms. Your approach must be to increase your hand action to get your clubhead speed to a level where your arms and shoulders don't have to supply that extra percentage of effort. Most golfers don't make any progress because they are more interested in taking out of their golf swings what is bad than putting in what is fundamentally correct.

So, for the moment, concentrate on swinging with more hand speed and less arm speed. For most golfers, in this particular stage of development, there is no such thing as a passive release. You must learn to use your hands to release the angle and turn the clubface over. As you progress, that release will happen more naturally at the proper time.

STAGE II DRILLS

Chair drill

Sitting in a chair or on a stool, hold your arms and club in front of you about chest-high, parallel with the ground. First swing the club back and forth, parallel to the ground, with your hands only. Hinge, unhinge and rehinge, letting the club turn over. Gradually incorporate your arm swing until you are swinging the club back to your right shoulder, then over to your left shoulder. This is excellent training for your hand and arm action.

The second stage of this drill is to actually hit balls off a tee with a 4- or 5-wood. Because there is little shoulder turn and no hip turn involved, this trains the arms to swing independently of the body.

Feet-together drill

Place your feet together—or no more than four or five inches apart—and assume your normal address position with the ball in the middle of your stance. Be sure you bend sufficiently at the hips and avoid the tendency to stand too close to the ball. Swing normally, starting with a 9-iron or pitching wedge and progressing to the longer clubs. Start with the ball on a tee and gradually lower it until it is on the ground. This drill promotes arms swinging and body following. Your feeling should be one of the hands and arms swinging down from the top before your body begins turning to the left, then your hands and arms swinging past your body and into the follow-through before your body turns far enough to face the target. The drill will reduce unwanted shoulder action, reduce tension in the arms and upper body and promote better balance, proper body action and better footwork.

Back-to-target drill

This drill is designed to promote the proper cocking and rotating of the hands, forearms and clubface. It will help you appreciate that you don't have to rotate your body excessively to square the clubface. It lets you experience hitting shots with the correct right-to-left shape while your body stays turned. It also forces the necessary folding of the left arm at the elbow after impact. The drill is done by standing with your feet at right angles to the target line, the ball teed opposite your toes at a point where you can reach it with your club as you turn your shoulders and square them as much as possible to the target line. Then simply cock your hands and swing your arms upward on the backswing. You will have no concern about swinging your arms around your body, because your body is already turned. Then let your arms swing down and strike the ball, letting the right arm cross over the left while the left elbow folds. Recock the club through impact while your torso stays turned to the right of the ball and target line. If the drill is done correctly, the ball will start to the right and hook back on target.

Tee drill

This is designed primarily to create the proper angle and swing plane. Stick a tee in the butt end of your grip. Make a half swing. On the backswing, make sure the tee points directly at the ball. On the follow-through, make sure the tee points at your divot mark. When the tee points inside of your target line on the backswing, your shots generally will fade. When it points outside, you generally will hit a draw. Only when the tee points along the target line will the shot be relatively straight.

Left-arm-only drill

This is an extension of the left-hand-only drill, done with a fuller range of motion in your later stages of development. Again starting with the ball on a tee, then gradually lowering it, cock the left hand and swing the left arm half or three-quarters of the way through your backswing, then clip the ball off the tee. Be sure to swing the club back with your left hand and arm, not your body, but allow your body motion to provide support for the arm swing as you develop proficiency in this drill.

Right-arm-only drill

This is an extension of the right-hand-only drill, done the same as the left-arm-only drill with the opposite hand and arm. Be sure you swing the club with your hand and arm, supporting that swing with your body as you go through a fuller range of motion.

Inside-loop drill

This drill differs from the ball-back drill in that it should be used if you already have good rotary action of your body. Scratch the loop shown in the picture in the ground with a club, or just visualize it. Position the ball in the center of your normal stance with a middle iron. As you swing, your feeling should be that the club stays along the line of play longer during the takeaway, moves around and up to the top of the backswing, then stays inside that backswing path longer into the downswing. The club should not be on the line of play until it strikes the ball. Your swing will be inside-to-outside the line, again with good rotation through impact. The drill counterbalances an ingrained outside loop and should be used if you take the club to the outside because of incorrect hand and wrist action as opposed to incorrect body rotation. Instead of feeling your hands bowing upward at the top, you should feel them cupping downward and inward.

THE INSIDE PATH PROGRAM
STAGE III: MASTERING THE PIVOT

...OF THE BODY THAT SUPPORTS THE FIRST AND SECOND SWINGS

WHAT TO DO

This is the most critical stage of development in creating your full golf swing. In this stage you swing your arms and hands through their maximum range of motion and incorporate the movement of the body—the pivot and the action of the legs—to allow and support that swinging. You build in the correct turning of the shoulders and hips, leg action, footwork and weight transfer, creating the proper big-muscle movement and support for the full swinging motion of the small muscles. With the ball on the ground, use the same four clubs as in Stages I and II, progressing to a driver with the ball on a tee in the final portions of Stage III when you can consistently control the other clubs.

HOW TO DO IT

Beginning with your feet six inches apart and the ball off your right toe, work on the maximum swinging of your hands and arms and the trunk rotation that allows it. Gradually widen your stance, adding a bigger pivot that incorporates correct trunk rotation and the leg and footwork that creates weight transfer and causes the movement of the lower body to complement your arm motion. Eventually you will end up with the full golf swing, all parts moving correctly.

As you learned in Stage II, ball position at address is critical because it allows you to develop the correct right-to-left ball flight. With the ball off the right toe you are forced to strike it on a path coming from the inside. And because your shots would continue to sail right if you did not square the clubface, you are forced to work on the rotation of your hands and arms.

Initially, you still will be hitting the low draw you saw in Stage II. As you become more accomplished at swinging from the inside and rotating the

Stage III: Swing the arms fully

At the beginning of Stage III, swing the arms to almost their
full range of motion, with the lower body responding
passively in a supporting role.

clubface, and as you progress to longer clubs, you will find that you are starting the ball too far to the right and having to hook it back too much to the left. At this point, start inching the ball forward to lessen both effects. At the end of Stage III you probably will be playing the ball off the middle of your stance and achieving a shot pattern that starts slightly to the right of your target and draws slightly back onto the target. But the ability to move the ball in this right-to-left fashion is always your criterion for changing the ball position.

Now that you are getting ready to swing your arms to their fullest extent, you should start thinking about pace, because your swing now will be long enough that pace becomes more important and you have more time in the swing to work with it. You should begin to feel a uniformity of grip pressure and arm pressure during your swing. You should start to feel more time being occupied in the change of directions at the top.

At this point, with your feet still relatively close together, you must maintain a pace far below what your ultimate swing speed will be. You cannot swing too hard because your lower

Actively incorporate the lower body

As you progress through Stage III, the lower body comes more actively into play to provide support for the swinging of the arms.

body, which at this point is still reacting fairly passively to the swinging of your arms, will not give enough support for a hard swing. Consequently you will go out of control if you try it. It's like driving a car on ice—your tires will provide enough traction or support if you go slowly, but if you want to speed up you had better go to studded tires or you will skid out of control. Later in Stage III you will train your lower body to provide support, so that in Stage IV you can enjoy the luxury of swinging your arms at 100 percent speed under control. But for now, swing only at 60 to 70 percent of what you feel is your maximum speed.

Perhaps most important of all as you begin your work in this area, you should start thinking about "feel."

Identify the feeling of the various motions you are making. The ideal way to play golf is simply with a total feel for the swing and no mechanical thoughts. It's impossible to play that way, of course, when you're involved in mechanics, as you are at the moment. But the sooner you begin to recognize and assimilate the feelings of a correct swing, the quicker and more completely you can reach your eventual goal.

Before you begin developing your maximum arm swing, let's examine the correct turning of the shoulders and hips that allows such a swing. If your shoulders do not turn fully, you obviously cannot swing your arms back fully. Ideally you want the shoulders to be turned by the swinging of your arms, but if they are resisting because of tension or because you are trying to manipulate them independently—and incorrectly—you must train them to operate properly. Remember, the shoulders turn. They do not tilt. They turn on a plane perpendicular to the spine. So if your spine is tilted in the proper address position, your shoulders won't turn on a plane horizontal to the ground. They may appear to be tilting, but they'll actually be turning at right angles to the spine.

There are three ways you can turn your shoulders, one of which is far better than the other two. You can turn your right shoulder behind your left, which is wrong and leads to a reverse weight shift. You can turn both shoulders around your spine, which is better. Ideally, you should feel that your left shoulder is turning in front of the right, which helps create a better weight transfer. An excellent way to identify this feeling of a correct shoulder turn is to stand erect, with your spine vertical, put your arms out in front of you at shoulder height and swing them back and forth around your body.

That's the feeling of turning you should have when your spine is tilted in the correct address position. If you relax your shoulders and let the swinging of your arms pull them around, this will happen naturally. Given correct posture and spine tilt at address, your arms should swing on a more upright plane than your shoulders. Your hands will be above your

shoulders at the top of your swing. Don't do anything to get in the way of this. The hands and arms will have swung on their correct plane, which you learned in Stage II, the shoulders will have turned correctly and everything will be right with the world at this point.

The hips are caught between the rock and the hard place, at the mercy of both the shoulders and the legs. They will react to the turning of the shoulders and to the action of the legs on both the backswing and the forward swing, unless you prevent this reaction with too much tension or a too-wide stance. But it's important for you to know *how* the hips should turn so you can identify the correct feeling. While the hips turn only about half as far as the shoulders, the sensation should be the same. You should feel that the left hip is turning toward a point where the right hip started while the right hip is turning back, away from the target line. There should be no lateral motion or sliding of the hips to the right.

The turning of your shoulders and hips provides the trunk rotation that, along with the lower-body action and weight transfer that we will discuss later, results in the proper pivot. A common problem among golfers at the higher-handicap levels is that in turning their upper body they do so without transferring their weight, or else in transferring their weight they do so without turning either the upper or lower body and end up swaying into an awkward and ineffective position.

How far should your shoulders turn? Basically as far as the swinging of your arms pulls them around, and that will be a result of your flexibility. The standard guideline is that the shoulders should turn 90 degrees, or until your back is facing the target, but that will depend on your physical structure.

Which brings us to the full arm swing. How far is full? As I discussed earlier, the full swing is basically how far you can get your arms and the club back without breaking down excessively at the left elbow or left wrist. You may be able to get your hands back to 10 o'clock or 12 o'clock. Whatever it is, accept that as your full swing at this stage.

As you begin to work on swinging your arms to the maximum, keep in mind that this is a continuation of Stage II. Your hands still control your arms, still control the takeaway of the club. The amount of hand action in a small swing and a full swing is the same. You want to feel that you should hinge your hands immediately at the start of the backswing, unhinge them through impact and hinge them again on the follow-through. But, whereas in Stage II you felt as if you were using a two-part swing, in Stage III you want to blend those two parts into a rhythmic, flowing motion back and forward. The hands are still setting the angle and the arms are still transporting the hands, but it becomes a smooth, unified action. This transition will not be as difficult as it might seem.

You know that your arms are going to be asked to do more work, to carry the club farther, and they will respond to this stimulus from the brain by going into action sooner. If you simply pay attention to the hands-arms back, arms-hands forward sequence, you'll get the necessary blending in both directions.

If you have ever had a chance to watch Tom Watson play golf, you have seen the perfect example of the motion I'm describing. Watson's hand action and arm swing are so smooth and unified that it appears he has a one-piece takeaway—indeed, Tom has even said that he takes everything away together. But closer inspection belies this. His clubhead moves considerably back before his arms change position, which means he is controlling the takeaway with his hands. He also is very firm at the top of his swing. You don't see him set the angle, because he has already begun to set it at the instant of takeaway. That's why, even though he is a fast swinger, he can spend a considerable percentage of his swing time making the change of direction. The club is in control, not bouncing around getting set late.

That's also why Watson, a relatively small man, can hit the ball so far. He has strong hands and forearms and he uses those speed-producing muscles correctly to produce a great distance.

As you begin building your full arm swing, remember always to keep the club on plane. Continue to use the tee drill that we discussed in Stage II to check this. It is only now, as you swing the left arm back as far as you can, that the tee in the end of your club will not be pointing at the target line throughout. At the top, assuming you can swing the club back to where it is parallel to the ground, the tee and the butt of your club should be pointing directly away from the target. But if you were to envision a plane extending upward from the ball through the tops of your shoulders, the tee and the club would still be on that plane at the top of your backswing and at the finish of your follow-through.

It is important to understand that the arms work in mirror images. The left arm remains basically straight going back while the right arm folds at the elbow. In the follow-through the right arm is straight while the left arm folds. This folding is necessary to accommodate the fact that the two arms are separated by the width of the shoulders. Because the club is closer to the right shoulder on the backswing, if the right arm didn't fold under the left, you would get stuck and cut off your backswing. For the same reason, the left arm must fold under the right on the follow-through or you would get too much rotary action of the body, a spinning to the left, combined with a scooping action. Too many golfers, pursuing the myth of "extension," try to keep their left arm on top, in a dominant position, during the follow-through. This prevents the club from coming back properly to the inside and reduces their clubhead speed and their ability to hit solid and straight shots.

Let's talk for a moment about rotation, where you want it and where you don't want it. Where you *don't* want it is in your shoulders and hips too soon. As you reach the top of your backswing and start down, you should feel your shoulders being contained, remaining turned while the arms swing down and forward on a slightly more inward path than the one on which they swung up. As you cultivate this feeling you also will be containing the hip turn, thus giving your arms a chance to swing into the ball from the inside.

Where you *do* want rotation is in the forearms and hands during the couple of feet on either side of the ball. In a good player's swing, the clubface is pointing to the right of his target well into his downswing. In that last couple of feet before impact, the rotation of his forearms and hands squares the face and gets his shot started on line. But that can be accomplished only if the club has started downward and inward on the forward swing and is approaching the ball on an inside path. If you rotate with your shoulders and hips during the change of directions, you throw the club to the outside and end up with reverse rotation through impact as you instinctively try to save the shot. Usually, it is beyond salvation.

So your feeling should be that the left arm crosses over the right going back and the right arm crosses over the left through impact, the elbows and wrists allowing the forearms and hands to rotate.

The biggest problem with most players is that they create too much rotation with the body, thereby taking control of the swing away from their hands and arms. So, contain the shoulders, swing your arms down from the inside and rotate your forearms and hands to create the right-to-left action you want in your shots.

Have you admired the long, free follow-through that most good players display, as opposed to the jerky, out-of-balance cut-off motion with which the majority of higher-handicappers finish their swings? Now that you are developing a full swinging of the arms, that professional-looking follow-through can be yours, too, if you follow three simple dictums:

1. You must be relatively free of tension as you swing through impact and into your follow-through.

2. You must be willing to let the angle re-form after impact . . . let the club pass your hands and keep going after you strike the ball.

3. You must allow the right heel to release from the ground and the lower body to turn freely to the target as you finish your swing.

Which brings us to the final building block in your golf swing. When you can consistently identify the correct sensations in your arms and upper body while swinging with your feet close together, and if your shots are consistently flying in the right-to-left

pattern you want, it is time to start widening your stance. Once you do that, your lower body comes actively into play.

The first thing to learn is how posture affects what you can or can't do with the lower body. For example, if your weight is too much on your left side at address, you won't be able to move your lower body properly. The key is to establish your weight distribution at address according to the amount of leg action you will need in your swing. The more you want the legs to work, the more you should set your weight on the right side at address. With the driver, which requires probably the maximum leg action, you should set as much as 55-60 percent of your weight over your right leg. For a short-iron or middle-iron shot, up to about a 5-iron, your weight should be evenly distributed because the leg action is not as dramatic. The only time your weight should be set left at address is for a short pitch or chip or a special low shot.

Remember my admonition earlier in the book against too much knee flex at address. If your knees are flexed too much, their tendency will be either to straighten through the shot or to fight against that straightening. In any event, they won't be making that down-and-forward move you want through the shot, so the action of the knees and legs will be in conflict with the swinging of the arms. So flex the knees just slightly at address, only enough to unlock them and break the

It's still inside-to-inside

In this stage, as always, the swing is still
inside-to-inside through impact and into the
follow-through.

tension in your legs.

The action of the knees is symmetrical to the swing path, in this case the inside-to-inside path you want to develop. During the backswing the right knee provides the foundation for your rotation but remains relatively stationary. The left knee moves to the right and forward. If your swing were to continue back far enough, the left knee would continue to move right and would go inward, emulating the swinging of your arms, but because the upper body turns more than the lower, it does not do this. On the forward swing, the left knee does not follow the same path it took on the backswing. The shape of the movement is the same in reverse, but it is more elongated. The left knee moves forward—to the left—and a bit outward toward the target for a slightly longer span, although it stays inside the path it took on the backswing. Then it rotates and moves away from the target line. That's because of the more active use of the legs—the leg drive—going forward to support the swinging of the arms.

The right-knee movement on the forward swing is similar to that of the left, to a point. In conjunction with the movement of the left, the right moves laterally and slightly outward toward the target line. Then it rotates as you swing into the follow-through, but it does not move back inside.

Your knee action on the backswing ideally is reactive. On the forward swing you may have to actively emphasize it until you build a feel for it into your swing.

Footwork on the backswing also should be mainly reactive, although you may have to consciously work at developing it if your feet aren't working well. As the turning of your upper body begins to pull your leg around, your left foot rolls inward, bending at the ankle. Then the left heel moves upward and to the right. The right foot remains stationary, but as the backswing continues your weight moves toward the heel. On the forward swing, the left heel is replanted and the weight rolls from the flat of your foot to the outside and from toe to heel as you swing through. Simultaneously, the right foot moves exactly as the left did on the backswing, except in the opposite direction. Your weight rolls to the inside of the foot and from heel to toe with the right heel coming up. As I explained earlier, don't push off the right foot too soon or you might create too much rotary action of the body and throw your swing to the outside.

At this time, simply try to tie the swing together by feeling that the feet and legs pick up the rhythm of the hands and arms in the backswing and the hands and arms pick up the rhythm of the feet and legs in the forward swing.

When you first bring the lower body into play with your pitching wedge, widen your stance only slightly. As you work with each successively longer club, gradually widen your stance until, with the driver, you are at normal width—the balls of your feet underneath the shoulder sockets.

When you do go to the driver, don't make the common mistake of swinging too hard. Most players can keep their swing under control with a 3-wood or 4-wood because those aren't the ultimate distance clubs. They still have the driver to rely on. But once they get a driver in their hands there is no artillery left and they feel they have to provide more effort to get the ball to go as far as they want it to. But for now, with your lower body action still not fully developed, swinging harder will only throw you out of control. Maintain that 60-70 percent swing speed I mentioned earlier. If you cannot emotionally control your swing speed with the driver, leave it in the bag until your development is further along in Stage IV.

WHAT YOU LEARN

At this stage of your development, you have created all the parts of the golf swing—but at the moment all you have are parts. The hands are hinging at the wrists, as you learned in Stage I. The arms are swinging from the shoulders, as you learned in Stage II. Now, in Stage III, the turning of the shoulders and hips and the action of the feet and legs have been added to provide big-muscle support for the small-muscle swinging.

You now know how to execute all those parts of your swing. This is the stage to which you should return when you suspect some part of your swing needs improving.

Now you are ready to advance to Stage IV, in which you will learn to tie all the parts together with proper preparation and timing. Finally, you will refine your swing so you can execute all the different shot shapes and trajectories that will make you a complete striker of the ball.

Ball-toss drill

Position yourself to the ball as you normally would for a pitching wedge, then a middle iron, then a driver. Only this time you have another golf ball in your right hand (left if you are a left-hander) instead of a club. Then make a backswing and throw the ball in your hand, trying to strike the ball on the ground. This drill is designed to train the body to release the club properly. It promotes the correct relationship between hand, arm and body and promotes proper use of the right hand and arm to release and turn over rather than release and cup upward. It also illustrates timing in the sense that as you stand farther from the ball on the ground, you must release the ball in hand sooner to hit your target.

Ball-back drill

With a 5-, 6- or 7-iron, assume your normal address posture and position the ball opposite your right heel. This automatically will open your clubface slightly and close your shoulders slightly. You will feel that your right arm is set inside and under the left arm. Then swing, the club approaching the ball from the inside, making sure you rotate your hands and arms to turn the blade over through impact. The drill will promote more rotary action of the body in the backswing and will help you feel that the rotary action to the left is contained longer into the downswing. It is also designed to give you the feeling of a descending blow with the clubface rotating through impact.

113

Left foot—right toe drill

This drill helps develop the feeling of your hands and arms swinging down from the inside, decreasing the rotary action of your body and increasing the rotation of your hands and arms. Position the ball just inside your left heel. Put all your weight on your left foot, place your right toe a foot or so behind your left heel in line with the ball and use it only for balance. Because the ball is to the right of your left foot, your body will be turned slightly to the right. This allows your body to turn to the right on the backswing but inhibits premature rotation to the left on the forward swing, forcing your hands and arms to swing down from the inside. Make only a half or three-quarter swing. You will develop the sensation that your hands and arms are swinging in front of and past your body as you rotate and square the clubface through impact, resulting in the correct right-to-left ball-flight. If your body rotates excessively, you will lose your balance and topple over.

Right foot—left toe drill

Once you have learned to make a swing from the inside with your clubface turning over, you can use this drill to help you get your swing path going more down the line and straighten your ball-flight. Position the ball just to the left of your right heel, put all your weight on your right foot and position your left toe a foot or so behind your right heel, directly in line with the ball. Make a half- to three-quarter swing. Done properly, this drill will give you the sensation of your arms swinging past your body and going left after impact. Once you develop enough arm freedom from doing the left foot—right toe drill, you can use this drill in conjunction to develop the correct inside-to-inside swing path.

Right-hand-off-after-impact drill

This drill teaches the lead arm to pace the trailing arm, as well as coordinating the movements of the upper and lower body. It will reduce excessive rotation of the shoulders by making you conscious of the paramount role your arms play in swinging the club. To do it, make a normal swing and just let the right hand slip off the club *after* impact. At the beginning, hit a few balls and let the right hand come off during the follow-through, then gradually sooner until it lets go just after impact. You'll soon get the feeling of pace and extension by the left side that you need.

115

THE INSIDE PATH PROGRAM
STAGE IV: MASTERING THE TIMING

...THAT WILL ALLOW YOU TO SWING WITH THE CORRECT SPEED-PRODUCING MUSCLES ON THE CORRECT INSIDE PATH

WHAT TO DO

In Stage IV you reach the pinnacle of hand, arm and body motion—whatever your pinnacle may be. You will learn to use your individual ability to its maximum potential by taking all the parts of your swing and blending them into a whole, refining your full-motion swing by improving its sequence and timing. You will develop the relationship between the big and small muscles to achieve your maximum clubhead speed with control. Finally, you will learn to adjust your ball position and your swing path to produce the different ball flights you will need to play to your potential.

HOW TO DO IT

You begin blending the parts together by establishing a preshot routine. The basics are simple—you identify and visualize the shot you want to make, then work back from the target to the ball to the body in setting up to make that shot. Specifically, after picking out your target or the line on which you want the ball to start, you aim your clubface behind the ball to that target, then align your body in relation to the clubface. Then waggle and go.

The important factor in building your routine is that you do it the same way every time and at the same pace, the same elapsed time. This sets up a rhythmic sequence that carries over into your swing and allows it to function in the same smooth rhythmic fashion.

The waggle is a vital part of your preshot preparations. It previews your swing and gets it started. It's always interesting to me to see tour players who say they start the swing with their arms waggle the club with their hands.

116

If they start the swing with their arms, why don't they waggle with just their arms? The reason is that most of them take the club away with their hands, whether they realize it or not. Most of the sensitivity we have available to feel the clubhead and swing path is lost when the shoulder, arm, wrist and hand become locked in a tense one-line relationship.

Your waggle should be the take-away move you first began to use in Stage I. Waggle the club away from and back to the ball with your hands and wrists only. Swing it back along your intended swing path and hinge your hands fully. When you first start working on your waggle—and it requires practice like everything else—take the club back so it is parallel with the ground, because a waggle that long is the best way to check if you are taking the club back on the correct path. Later you might want to reduce the length a little, although I recommend you make your waggle quite full. And make it without tension, free and easy, the way you want to swing. The length of the waggle will vary, of course, with different clubs as you preview the length of swing and length of shot you are going to make. With the driver it will be quite long, with the pitching wedge less than half as long.

Always make the waggle without tension, free and easy, the way you want to swing. The number of waggles you make before each shot is an individual preference, although I like to limit it to a couple to avoid standing over the ball too long. Whatever number is comfortable for you, make that same number every time.

At the same time you are waggling with your hands, you should be "waggling" with your feet and legs to relax and prepare your lower body for action. I find that alternately tapping my heels on the ground as I waggle the club breaks the tension and induces the feeling of lightness I want in my legs when I start the swing.

When you start working on tying together your swing, remember first to check your ball position. In Stage IV your guideline is to position the ball in the center of your stance with all irons, just slightly ahead of center with the fairway woods. With the driver, you can start by placing the ball two inches or so ahead of center. Eventually you want to get it as far forward as possible and still be able to swing into the ball from the inside.

To tie the feet and legs together with the hands and arms in your swing, your sensation should be that they are acting in concert. If the hands and arms aren't working properly, the feet and legs won't work properly and vice versa. In the refined swing, the hands and arms are complemented by the feet and legs going back and the feet and legs are complemented by the swinging of the hands and arms going forward.

An analogy might be dancing a waltz or fox-trot or jitterbug with a partner. The feet provide support and move you around the dance floor

117

while your arms guide your partner, but both actions are done with rhythm to the same beat.

Your initial task is to train your lower body to move at the right time. You should feel as if you are pushing off your left foot as soon as the clubhead starts back. As your hands move, your left foot should roll inward off the ankle and upward from the heel. There will be a corresponding movement of the left knee to the right which synchronizes with the movement of the arms. While your feeling should be that the hands and feet are starting together, the outward appearance will be that the hands and arms will be leading. This is only because the hands and the arms can move faster than the feet and legs and so seem to be outreaching them.

On the backswing, the right foot and leg are relatively stationary, but on the forward swing both feet and legs act in concert with the downward swinging of the arms and hands. The first move out of the top should be the simultaneous replanting of the left heel and a pushing off of the inside of the right foot while the arms start inward and downward.

Done in concert, these movements back and through will smooth out your sequence and give you the timing you need to swing on the inside path and create sufficient speed to give you long, on-target shots. Working with the accompanying drills will help you tie the upper and lower body actions together.

While you are practicing, be sure to keep checking your swing plane with the tee in the butt end of your club, noting the correct positions I described earlier throughout the backswing, at the top and at the finish.

Also make sure your swing path matches your clubface alignment. In other words, if your clubface is aimed to the right, as it will be while you are playing the ball back of center in your stance, swing to the right. Don't aim the clubface right and swing left or vice versa unless you are trying to hit some of the special shots that we'll discuss later.

In further refining your swing along the guidelines I have laid out in the previous stages, be aware that while the mechanical action of the parts is important, the sequence in which you put those parts together is even more important. The particular speed or pace of your swing is not important, as long as excessive speed doesn't cause you to go out of control. Some players naturally swing faster than others. There is no such thing as too fast as long as the sequence is correct, as long as you are doing the right things at the right places at the right time. For example, Tom Watson's golf swing is faster than most, but it is not too fast for his strength. Many golfers blame swinging too fast for their troubles when faulty sequence really is the culprit. If a person thinks his swing is too fast and tries to slow the whole thing down but still has the wrong sequential movement, all he has really done is slow down a bad swing.

In the long run, sequence is something that must be felt. All the mechanical parts working to perfection won't accomplish a thing unless they work together in the correct sequence and unless you can identify the *feel* of that sequence. You should feel that your hands and arms swing away at the same time as the feet and legs while the body pivots or turns to accommodate that swing. Your shoulders should feel passive during the change of direction, remaining turned while the feet and legs start forward as the arms swing inward and downward. With the correct sequence, you will get the feeling that your arms unwind the body as you swing through impact. When I hit what I consider a perfectly struck shot, I get the sensation that the clubhead has contacted the ball on-center while my hands are racing to catch up the clubhead, my arms are racing to catch up to my hands and my shoulders are racing to catch up to my arms and hands. You should cultivate the same sensation.

Remember, good timing is a product not only of proper sequential movement but also of spending the correct percentage of time in the various positions. Continue to work, as you did in Stages II and III, on spending the right amount of time at the right place, especially during the critical change of direction, so your sequence will work correctly.

As you progress through Stage IV, by working with the full-swing thoughts you've been given and with the accompanying drills, you will find that the correct sequence changes slightly. To this point you have been trying to make the forward action of the legs simultaneous with the inward and downward swinging of the arms. Ultimately, however, the movement of the lower body becomes a reaction to the support required for the speed of the upper body movement. So as your swing improves and you advance from the 60 or 70 percent effort to a faster swing, or a longer swing in the case of the longer clubs, you will anticipate the increased speed of your arms and your feet and legs will start to work sooner during the change of direction. They have to do that to accommodate the faster swinging of the arms.

The earlier and faster movement of the lower body accentuates the swinging of the arms on the inside path. It helps contain the rotary movement of the shoulders and hips while allowing you to swing your arms faster and longer on the inside path.

That's why you hear good players say they hit the ball farther by using a stronger, faster leg drive. But they're really not hitting it farther with their legs. They're simply moving their feet and legs faster to support the increased speed of their arm swing.

Once you can achieve consistent on-center contact and a consistent right-to-left ball flight with all your clubs, including the driver, while swinging at a reduced rate of speed, you can begin

Stage IV: All parts work together, legs supporting arms

At this point everything works together, the hands moving the clubhead, the arms carrying the hands in rhythmic fashion through the swing as the lower body provides passive support on the backswing and active support on the forward swing, moving laterally and then in rotary fashion to accommodate the motion of the arms.

to speed up the movement of your feet and legs and hands and arms. Do it gradually, always keeping your swing under control. When your on-center contact or your ball flight begins to deteriorate, slow down until it improves. Then you can move forward again.

As your lower body action improves and your swing speeds up, the fact that the club is staying on the inside path longer will cause your swing path to be too much in-to-out and you'll find your shots will be starting too much to the right and probably too low. You'll reach a point where too much hand-arm rotation is required to hook the ball back on target. Now refer to your ball position, gradually inching the ball forward until you get the trajectory and shape to your ball flight you want with your swing speed of the moment.

The final adjustment in your ball position will depend primarily on how well you use your feet and legs. The ultimate would find you positioning the ball opposite your left heel with the driver while retaining your ability to strike the ball from the inside. But you may find you can't play the ball that far forward. As soon as you begin to swing from the outside with too much rotary action and the ball starts left, you'll know you have it too far forward and must adjust it back until you are once again swinging on the inside path.

Whatever that position is for you, you now will be at the point where

you can achieve maximum clubhead speed. As I indicated earlier, you can swing the club faster in a circle than you can on a straight line. This means your ideal swing path is inside to inside or, more specifically, inside to along the line at impact and back to the inside.

At this stage your swing should begin to feel more circular and less lateral. You should feel your left arm moving left, away from the target line, and more around your body after impact. If you look at the finish position of such great ball strikers as Ben Hogan, Sam Snead, Lee Trevino and many others, you will see that the club ends up more horizontal than vertical, behind them and pointing to the right rather than down to the ground. This indicates their swing through and past the ball has been *around* the body rather than up and out toward the target. Once you begin to ingrain this feeling into your swing and you are still getting your desired ball flight, you will know your ball position is correct and you have the best chance to hit it as far as *you* possibly can.

You now have reached the stage in your swing development where you should be able to create all kinds of ball flights with very simple adjustments in ball position and setup. For instance:

To hit a low draw, play the ball back in your stance, your clubface aimed slightly to the right. Your swing path will be from the inside and your hands and forearms should react to the clubface position and rotate to close it, creating the right-to-left flight of the ball.

To hit a high, soft draw, play the ball slightly farther back than normal, set your weight a bit more to the right at address and feel you are staying more behind the ball as you swing normally, allowing your hands and arms to rotate.

To hit a left-to-right fade, position the ball slightly forward of normal. Your clubface will be looking slightly to the left. Your swing will react by taking on a more "uppish" shape. You will swing into the ball more from the outside and you should have the feeling you are "holding on," allowing less rotation of the clubface through impact. Again, the ability to hit a low fade or a high fade is primarily the result of your weight distribution at address and body position relative to the ball at impact. The more your weight is set to the left and the more your body is centered on the ball at impact, the lower the shot. The more you are set to the right at address and are behind the ball at impact, the higher the ball will fly. Just remember that with a driver, because the ball is on a tee, you don't want to get your body ahead of the ball. That will cause you to make a descending blow that will pop the ball up.

Experiment with the various ball position and setup adjustments—with irons, fairway woods and the driver—to determine which combinations produce the desired ball flight for you.

Practice them until you are comfortable enough to use them on the course when the situation dictates.

You can hit draws or fades—relatively slight hooks or relatively slight slices—with the method I've just described. When you want to curve the ball excessively, to hit intentional hooks and slices, then you must go back to the ball-flight fundamentals we discussed in Chapter 2. The combination of swing path and clubface position at impact determines in which direction the ball starts and how it curves.

Thus you must preset your clubface and your stance if you want to hit a big curve around a tree or other obstacle. My rule of thumb for these shots is to aim your clubface at the spot where you want your ball to finish and set your stance along the line on which you want the ball to start. For example, to hit a hook, position the ball back in your stance, close or turn the blade to the left by aiming it at your eventual target and set your body to the right so you can swing along a path that will start the ball far enough to the right that it will miss the obstacle you are facing. For a slice, do just the opposite—play the ball a bit forward, open the clubface or turn it to the right by aiming at your target and set your stance left, again allowing sufficient room to clear the obstacle.

Remember that you don't have to make excessive arm and hand rotation to hook the ball or try extra hard to prevent rotation to slice it. You already have changed your hand position, in effect, by presetting the clubface, so all you have to do is make a normal swing. If you rotate excessively from a closed blade position, you will hit a smothered hook into the ground. If you hold on or fail to release sufficiently with an open clubface, you probably will knock the ball right into the tree you are trying to get around.

However, be aware that your instincts may cause you to hold a closed clubface open through impact. Conversely, you may react to an open clubface with excessive rotation that will start the ball too far left and reduce your intended slice.

The answer, again, is to make a normal swing, being sure your swing path matches your stance line. Then you will get the curve that puts your ball on target.

WHAT YOU LEARN
You now have worked through all the stages of development and consequently through all the stages of ball flight. In Stage I your ball went low and relatively straight, or maybe a bit to the right, for just a few yards, because you were swinging only with your hands. In Stage II your ball flight was definitely right to left and lower than normal with a swing in which you added some arm motion to your hand action. In Stage III, when you started to lengthen your swing, your first objective was to hit that same low right-to-left shot but farther because of

your increased motion. Before you left Stage III, however, you were able to hit the ball higher and also were beginning to learn to hit the ball relatively straight by moving it forward in your stance.

In Stage IV, everything has come together and you have learned to use your hands, arms and body to their maximum potential. You know how to swing at maximum speed with relatively little effort by using the correct muscles, and you know how to achieve all kinds of ball flight.

As I pointed out at the beginning, you can't learn it all in one day. You undoubtedly will progress and then regress before you progress again. It is permissible—even desirable—to fluctuate back and forth among the stages during your learning process, reinforcing what you have learned before and then returning to what you are trying to learn.

That's why I find the stage concept so appealing. Whether you are a learner or an accomplished player, any time your swing begins to deteriorate you can go back through the stages and find where you need work. That way you can get your swing back in tune more quickly and keep it there longer.

One final word on stages—no matter what your level of proficiency, you can and should play golf in different stages at different times. I don't think you should ever play an entire round of golf in one stage, because you are always facing different situations that require different shots and different swing stages.

For example, on the early holes of a tournament round, my golf swing is certainly more Stage III than Stage IV. If the truth were known, it probably feels like Stage II, because I am trying to achieve control to breed confidence.

I'd suggest you try to play with the same feeling earlier in the round. As you develop your confidence, composure and control as the round goes on, your swing can begin to move to a more aggressive, Stage IV level. But if you come to a really tight hole, you might want to drop back to Stage III for that situation. You have to be flexible enough and aware enough to use all stages as you progress through the round.

STAGE IV DRILLS

Baseball drill

This two-stage drill helps create the proper timing relationship between the upper body and lower body. To begin with, take your normal address position. Now move your left foot back next to your right foot, moving the clubhead back the same distance. From there, swing back and, as you swing forward, move your left foot to the left and put it back where it started.

Here's the second stage. Start from your normal address position. As you swing back, let your left foot come off the ground, swing back and touch your right ankle while you are completing your backswing. Then replant your left foot in the same place and swing forward.

Swish drill

Use an old shaft without a head or simply turn a club upside down and grip it at the hosel for this one. Swing and try to create the loudest possible "swish" through the impact area. Do it with the left arm only, the right arm only and then both arms. This drill promotes retaining the arm-shaft angle longer on the forward swing instead of casting the club with your hands from the top. It develops a feeling of lightness and trains your muscles to work at top speed during the swing.

127

CHAPTER · 7

TROUBLE-SHOOTING

HOW TO FINE-TUNE YOUR SWING—HOW TO CORRECT IT WHEN THINGS GO WRONG

The development program in the preceding chapters will teach you to swing correctly on the inside path, to use the proper muscles to create your maximum swing speed and to use the parts of your body to support and enhance that speed.

This chapter, now, will provide you with the means to fine-tune your swing and will serve as a trouble-shooting guide when things start going wrong in your development. For example, when I run into trouble with my own swing, I first check my address position, aim and alignment. After that I examine what I'm doing in my backswing, then in my forward swing. If I can't pinpoint the problem in those areas, I look for a whole-swing error, the shape of my swing, the allowances I must make in changing from club to club.

The following material is laid out in that fashion as I discuss what I consider to be the ideal swing and how the

parts of the body work and mesh together during that swing. During this discussion I'll dispel some common myths and misconceptions that may retard your development unless you rid your golfing mind of them.

Bear in mind that the swing you develop may not match this swing model because of your particular physical characteristics. But you should follow these concepts with a swing that fits your idiosyncracies. In the final portion of the chapter I'll suggest some adjustments you might want to make to adapt your physique, flexibility and level of talent to the model as much as possible. This will help you relate *your* development process to an overall picture of the ideal swing.

THE BACKSWING

When does the golf swing actually start? Technically, it doesn't start until the clubhead has started away from the ball with the intent of creating a backswing. But what about all that movement that goes on before that time—the waggle? In reality, the swing of the better player starts with that waggle, not with the first movement of the backswing. The better player develops a sense of rhythm with the waggle, and the backswing starts by picking up that rhythm to create a smooth transition from pre-swing positions to inswing movement.

The correct takeaway should begin with the hands moving the clubhead first, perhaps only barely perceptibly, but first nonetheless. A simple equation relating time to the rate of speed of movement times the distance to be covered will help you understand which takeaway and backswing is correct for you. The clubhead, grip, hands, arms and shoulders all travel different distances in the backswing. If the backswing is to be completed properly, then either the parts that travel the farthest must start earlier or they must move faster to finish at the same time as the parts that don't have as far to go. Either the clubhead, which has the farthest to travel, starts first or, out of necessity, it must travel a lot faster than the rest of the parts to make up the extra ground it has to cover. The analogy here would be the staggered start of the 440-yard race. Since the person on the outside lane has farther to travel, if the runners were all to start and finish at the same line, he would have to be Superman to ever win a race. So a staggered start is used, putting the outside-lane starting blocks forward to equalize the distance.

To the average player, starting the swing with a one-piece takeaway causes the clubhead to have to move so quickly during the last part of the backswing that the club is bound to end up out of control because of a lack of sufficient strength to stabilize the speed of the club at the top. If the golf swing were a one-lever motion then you could practice a one-piece takeaway, but to create proper distance and leverage with your swing, an angle must be formed between your arms and the clubshaft. The angle is set by the hinging or cocking of the hands. When you delay this action and the angle is set later in your backswing, unless you have extremely good pace and quite a lot of strength it will happen so abruptly that you will probably lose control of your swing. It is also a common tendency for the players who set the angle too late in the backswing to release the angle too soon in the forward swing, thus dissipating power and accuracy.

Once the hands start, and the wrists allow, the movement of the clubhead, the arms pick up the rhythm of the hands and clubhead and carry them around and up to the top of the backswing. It is the movement of the arms that masks the cocking of the wrists in the swing. *While the hands are trying to set the angle immediately, the swinging of the arms blends the hinging of the hands into the entire motion of the backswing. The sooner,*

Hand action: What you feel is not what you get

When you initiate the swing with your hands, your feeling may be that your hands alone are swinging the club back (A). But what happens is that the arms pick up the rhythm of the hands and clubhead, so that the immediate hinging of the hands is not as acute as you feel it is (B).

and faster, you move your arms in the takeaway, the later the hinging of the hands will occur. The later and slower you swing your arms, the earlier the angle will be formed. So, the early set or late set or swinging set of the golf club is determined not so much by just the quickness of the hands but by the relationship of your hand speed to the speed of your arm swing. When the speed of your hands and arms is about equal in the takeaway, then the hands will move faster near the top of the backswing. There is nothing innately wrong with this *if* you have the hand and wrist strength to control it. However, there will be far less strain placed on the smaller muscles of the hands and wrists if they are allowed to move earlier in the backswing.

At this point I would like to warn you of one of the most dangerous pastimes of the avid golfer—PICTURE READING! I'm convinced that more average golf swings have been hurt by still pictures than have been helped. Stop-action photography eliminates the most important aspect of the swing—motion. At one time in my development as a golfer, I thought my hands were helping me set the angle fairly early in the backswing. At least that's what I felt! I was shocked when I saw some pictures of my swing showing the angle hardly formed at the point in the swing where I felt it would be completed! After some closer examination, however, I realized that the later-than-expected formation of the angle was due to the swinging of my

arms, not the lack of use of my hands. My hands were doing what I felt they were doing, but the addition of my arms into the swing gave it a totally different outward appearance.

The purpose of the backswing is simply to put the club, along with your hands, arms and body, in a position that facilitates swinging on the proper inside swing path back to the ball. There is no power created in the backswing. When your motion is backward and around and then you have to change directions and go forward and around, any momentum of the club is lost because it has to come to a stop before it can start going the other way.

Any tension you build will make it difficult to get into the proper position at the top and will keep you from making as long a backswing as you might like. When muscles get tighter, they get shorter and don't have their normal range of motion. So, while you may feel a pulling sensation in the left side of your back and shoulders at the top, *the backswing should be kept as free of tension as possible.* Hale Irwin once described it as a "backplace," and that's probably as good a thought as any for you to have.

As I discussed in dealing with the address position, keeping the left arm straight can be overdone and contribute to excessive tension. A person who has a big range of motion with the arms can afford to keep the left arm straight. If you don't have that much range, you can let the left elbow relax a little. I'll tell you more about that later.

Fullness of motion aside, there is another important reason to keep the left arm from becoming stiff and locked on the backswing. It has to do with the rotation of the arms in the swing, along with the proper rotation of the clubface. When the left arm becomes locked at the elbow you eliminate just about any chance of getting any rotary action of your club, unless it comes from an overuse of some other part of your body, namely the hands, or in some cases the shoulders or hips.

In the chapter on how the clubface influences your swing and what happens at impact, I said that the worst possible position of the clubface in the backswing was to get it closed or hooded. When the left arm doesn't rotate over the right in the backswing, the backswing will become more lateral and especially vertical, hindering the rotary action. The clubface will most likely be closed and the combination of these things will most certainly serve to cut off the flow of your backswing. It's no coincidence that so many swings that are short, quick or jerky have been precipitated by a stiff left arm. Relax your arms, especially the left one, and let them swing back, around and finally up to a completely full backswing. Remember, for every player with a backswing that is too long and too loose, I see hundreds that are too short and too tight.

In keeping with freeing your arm

Be free of tension at top

At the completion of your backswing, the only tension you should feel is a stretching of the upper body muscles—your left arm should be relaxed, your left foot released from the ground and your weight over your right leg.

swing, the thought of keeping your right elbow tucked in—golfers once were advised to practice with a handkerchief tucked under the right armpit—serves only to tie your right arm to your right side on the backswing. In a sense, you are eliminating your right arm swing, and if you do that you do a pretty good job of eliminating your left arm swing, too, because they are both holding on to the same club. Having now effectively eliminated—or at least greatly hindered—the swinging of your arms, you are left with the need to produce excessive hand action as compensation. And because the arms are now tied to the turning of the body, you get too much rotary action in your swing.

In the swing shape I see in good players, the arms and hands appear to be moving away from the body halfway into the backswing. Halfway into the downswing they appear to be moving back in toward the body, and halfway through the follow-through they are moving away from the body again.

So don't be afraid to let your arms—and that includes your right elbow—swing away from your body to produce the necessary lateral and vertical aspects of your swing. A fellow named Jack Nicklaus has been accused for years of having a flying right elbow at the top of his swing, and he hasn't done badly at the game.

A complete backswing is one that is sufficiently long for the shot you are undertaking with the club you have in your hands. *The top of your swing should be the position from which you are able to generate the maximum amount of clubhead speed that you can control*—and I emphasize that a backswing without control is of little or no value.

The completed backswing will take on different appearances, depending on the shot you are trying to play. However, there are some common denominators regardless of what you're trying to do with the ball. In studying the simple act of throwing a ball, many things become obvious. First, the distance you want to throw the ball dictates how much arm swing you need. The length and speed of your arm motion determine how the bigger muscles of the legs and body will be used. One thing is apparent from the very beginning, however. The momentum of the body complements the motion of the throw . . . it does not interfere with it. There is a definite transfer of weight to the back leg when the arm is being cocked to throw the ball. This means that the right leg supports the flow of the backswing and thereby frees the left leg to become the support for the forward motion. The critical point of discussion here is that when distance is required, the throwing motion incorporates a two-axis movement for power. The same must occur in the golf swing. As your need for distance increases, there must be two axes in your swing. *The right leg should be the pivot for the backward motion, while the left leg assumes the same responsibility for the forward swing.*

At the top of your backswing for a full shot, the majority of your weight should be over your right leg. The weight doesn't have to stay inside your right leg, nor do you have to have the feeling that your head is still or "over the ball."

Too much golf instruction has centered around keeping your head still during the swing and avoiding a sway to the right on the backswing. Unfortunately, in pursuing this concept, too many players try so hard to avoid swaying to the right that they end up tipping their heads and upper bodies to the left—the so-called reverse weight shift. At this point they have destroyed the lateral aspects of their golf swing—instead of the club going back, around and up, it just goes in and up while the weight shifts to the left. From there all the weight can do is shift to the right on the forward swing, so the direction the body is moving is in conflict with the direction the club is moving in both stages of the swing.

I am not advocating that you sway, but if you are going to make an error one way or another I would rather you let your head move slightly to the right on the backswing and then time the motion back to the left on the forward swing. Then, at least, you have increased your body motion and put the momentum of your swing going in the right direction.

Also, when considering the completed backswing position, you must identify the correct position of the clubshaft. The ideal position for the shaft is perfectly parallel to the target line. "Pointing the club at the target" is a common phrase that we hear in conjunction with this point, but I have never liked that approach because it assumes correct aim and alignment, which is hardly ever the case with most players. Also, the club at the top is not pointing to the target but down a line parallel to the target line. The best check-point for the correct shaft position at the top is actually not at the top but halfway into the backswing. When your clubhead is approximately waist high, the shaft should be parallel to the target line. From this position the club should arrive to the correct place at the top of the backswing if the hands and arms maintain their relationship and continue swinging back and around properly.

THE DOWNSWING

Once the backswing has been completed, the next concern is the change of direction from backswing to downswing, without a doubt the most critical point in the swing. There has been a multitude of tips, tidbits and old wives' tales written to get this very complicated task accomplished simply. However, completeness must never be sacrificed for the sake of simplicity. *Each part of the body must be taught to work correctly to achieve consistency in the change of direction.* While one part may help another, you cannot expect one part to do the job of several parts. There is no one thought, one part of the body or one movement that will insure a cor-

135

Swing starts downward and inward

From these two views, we see that the swing starts downward and inward with the arms while the rotary action of the shoulders is contained and the lower body is moving laterally to support the flow of the forward swing.

rect and consistent transition from backswing to downswing for all players.

The truth is that how you start the downswing depends on your stage of development. The more accomplished player may feel the lower body initiates the forward swing, and this is probably true for him, but what the novice doesn't realize is that the better player first learned to control his upper body before he began using his lower body more actively.

The first objective when starting the forward swing is to insure that the club starts downward and inward, not outward and around. For this to happen, the rotary action of the body must be contained long enough to allow the hands and arms to start on the proper path down to the ball. The body must not interfere and cause the club to take an alternate route to the ball, from the outside.

Earlier in the book we talked about the three parts to the golf swing—the first swing, the second swing and the pivot of the body. We need all three throughout the swing. At no time can you sell one part down the river for any reason. For example, you may have heard the phrase "pull the club down from the top." This sounds safe enough, but if you pursue it you'll end up with the shoulders pulling *around* instead. You see, to be able to pull something you have to be in front of it, and at the top of the swing that translates to the shoulders. So instead of starting the forward swing with a downward movement, you start it with a rotary action, and that's the kiss of death—unless you happen to like the pulls and pull-slices that result. But even more important than the obviously misdirected path of the downswing, the left arm becomes locked to the left shoulder, thereby wiping out fully one-third of your speed capacity that comes from the free-swinging motion of the arms from the shoulders. If the shoulders pull the arms and the arms pull the club, when does this action stop to allow the clubhead to catch up with everything so it can be square at impact?

Ideally, the turning of the body in the backswing should be a reaction to the swinging of the arms. This same sequence should apply in the unturning of the body during the forward swing. The trunk of the body should react to the swinging of the hands and arms as well as the movement of the lower body. Before this can happen, however, the arms must be trained to swing downward and inward, and this means you must keep the shoulders passive at the beginning of the downswing.

After the hands and arms are trained to swing down from the inside, then the action of the lower body can become an asset. In fact, if you want to achieve your maximum distance potential, using your lower body correctly becomes a necessity. The use of the right leg as an axis on the backswing must be matched by using the left leg for the same purpose on the forward swing. Please understand that the proper use of the feet and legs can help to maintain the correct inside path of the club to the ball, but to use the legs to *create* that inside path is difficult at best without having trained the upper body first.

When the time comes for the legs and feet to actively participate in the golf swing, they should support and complement, not dominate. In the backswing they support and complement the correct pivot of the body, while in the forward swing they provide the necessary big-muscle control for the faster movement of the smaller muscles in the hands and wrists.

It is especially important to emphasize the supportive role of the bigger and stronger lower-body muscles. Halfway into the downswing the arms should be moving in toward the body to set up the proper inside swing path. But, if the upper body becomes dominant, its excessive rotary action will force the arms away from the body. So, in making the change of direction let the upper-body action be responsive to the correct path of the arms and movement of the lower body.

When the upper body stays "quiet" during this part of the swing, it is sometimes referred to as *staying behind the ball*. I would caution you to use care, however, in consciously trying to stay too far behind the ball with your upper body. This could cause more problems than it's worth.

Staying *behind* the ball on the forward swing is not nearly as important as staying *inside* the ball. It is too easy for a person to work on staying behind the ball, then let the upper body open up and swing the club into the ball from the outside. At the same time he is restricting his arm freedom. If anything, there are too many golfers who are behind the ball too much at impact. In most instances, that's because they never got behind the ball going back and are falling back on their right sides as a reaction.

Staying behind the ball should be a reaction to the flow and force of your legs, arms and club. Every action has an equal and opposite reaction. If you create enough forward flow of your legs, arms and hands as you swing them past your body, your upper body will want to counterbalance that so you will stay behind the ball sufficiently.

Given one choice or the other, I would prefer to be slightly past the ball but having contained the rotary action of the upper body than to stay behind the ball while letting the upper body rotate and open up, creating an outside path for the swing.

The momentum of the body should complement the motion of the swing, not interfere with it. Since the direction of the swing is downward and forward at this point, the sensation in your feet and legs also should be downward and forward. If you stay behind the ball and the motion of your body is upward and to the left because of the excessive rotary action of your body, there will be a conflict between your body movement and swing path.

From the change of direction through impact, the feet must provide traction for the force of the swing you are making. When this happens correctly there will be a feeling of downward pressure in your feet as a reaction to the downward force of the swing. If this lower body action is not present, the result will be a change in the shape of the movement of the club. For example, many golfers have the ruinous habit of keeping the left heel up while the swing is trying to move down through impact. The usual result is a swing that will move up and over the ball, usually causing the head to jerk up. The whole mess is written off to poor control of the head, but that's obviously not the case.

As you approach impact, the greatest rotation of the club is about to occur. If the swing path to the ball is correctly from the inside, the clubface will be pointing well to the right of the line of play just prior to impact, necessitating the "release" or rotary action to square it at impact.

Releasing or rotating the clubhead through the ball is ideal, but the thought of *trying* to get the clubhead through the ball might not be the best way to get it to happen. Just remember that before you can get *through* the ball, you must first get *to* the ball, and that means from the inside.

At impact, everything should be the result of movements made earlier in the swing. If you're thinking instead of reaction at impact, you're in trouble. Keep the club moving and flowing with as constant a grip pressure as possible, allowing the force of the swing to strike the ball, rather than trying to force the swing to hit the ball. Impact is not the time to try and develop more power. It is rather the time to allow the forces you have tried to contain to that point to be unleashed.

If I have a conscious thought at and through impact, it is to retain a sense of balance and ease that will allow me to maintain a reasonably steady swing center. I do not try to keep my head down, because I feel strongly that proper head action is the result of a proper swing. After all, my head is attached to my neck and that to my shoulders and so on—if my body loses its balance and fluidity and jerks all over the place, how can I expect to keep my head steady? Besides, if you try to keep your head down too long, you will cut off your follow-through, and all you'll be looking at is the divot in the ground—with the ball probably too close as well!

The same person who told you to keep your head down probably advises you also to make a high follow-through, and that's a classic myth. Nobody can keep his head down and make a high follow-through at the same time, because the two are totally incompatible.

The concept of a high follow-through itself is misleading. When most higher-handicappers pursue a high follow-through, they make it in *front* of the body, whereas all good players have a high follow-through *behind* or *around* the body. You may have seen pictures of Ben Hogan's classic follow-through, his left arm well left of his left shoulder, the club pointing to his right and almost parallel to the ground. Lee Trevino is another who finishes in this position, and every good player approximates that look to one degree or another.

The reason is the rotary action I've talked about through impact and beyond. The club strikes the ball coming from the inside, then swings back to the inside on the follow-through. Your right arm position at the finish of your swing should be a mirror image of your left arm position at the top of your backswing. How much around or behind your body you finish with your hands and arms depends, then, on how upright or flat your swing plane is, but in all cases the hands should finish to the left of your head and even left of your left shoulder.

When the higher-handicapper tries to make a high follow-through, he usually swings too vertically and eliminates the necessary rotary action. Often this is because he has used the rotary action too soon in his forward swing and must swing his arms and hands vertically to compensate. Otherwise he would fall on his butt.

So be aware that the high follow-through is really a full follow-through. Make the rotary action at the right time in your swing and allow your hands, arms and club to swing left and around your body after impact. Your hands and arms will finish in the correct position. You'll also probably hit a pretty good shot.

YOUR SWING SHAPE

What about the shape of your swing? Should you have an upright swing or a flat one, or what? The answer is not necessarily any of the above. You should have a swing that is on the *correct* plane, and that is different for each club in your bag. There is no such thing as one swing plane for everyone or even for every club. The shape and length of your swing must match the shape and length of the club you are using. That's correct—the shape and length of your swing must match the lie and the length of the club you are using.

Lie is simply the angle at which the clubhead is affixed to the shaft in relation to the ground. The shorter the club, the steeper or more upright will be the angle between the shaft and the ground when the clubhead is properly soled. The longer the club, the shallower or flatter will be that angle.

Let each club seek its own plane

Using the camera from different angles shows that each club is swung on a plane for that particular club, a plane largely determined by length of club and setup position. By repositioning the camera for the series at left, angling it from the ball through the throat for each club, it can be seen that the pitching wedge (top), 5-iron and driver all are on plane at the top of the swing. But by leaving the camera in the same position for the series at right, it is obvious that each of those planes is different, the club finishing flatter and farther from the target line the longer it gets. Again, this is predicated by the address position, but you should let it happen.

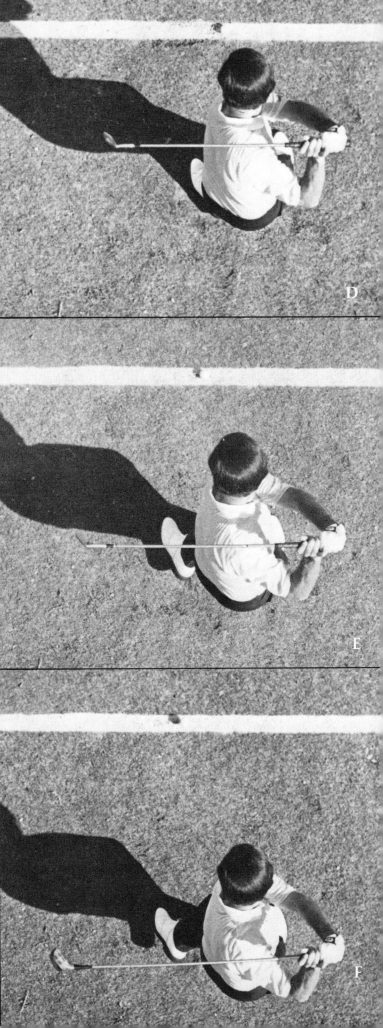

Thus, the flatter the lie of the club, the flatter or more around your body the swing shape must be. As the lie of the club becomes more upright, so must the shape of the swing become more upright. You can't make the same swing with a driver at a ball teed in the air and with a pitching wedge at a ball nestled in the grass.

At the same time, the shorter the club in your hands, the shorter your swing should be. With a driver you want as long a swing as possible, so long as you can keep it under control, because you need to generate more clubhead speed for maximum distance. Also, your target area is much bigger. You usually have a fairway 30 to 40 yards wide in which to put your ball. But as you move down to the shorter irons, your shots must be much more precise. You have little need for power but must be more accurate, because now you are aiming at the hole or a small area of the green. So your swing must be shorter to give you maximum control.

These changes in your swing, especially in its shape, need not be made consciously. They will happen as a result of the change in your stance and posture to accommodate the various club lengths. I'll discuss that in a moment. But it's extremely important to be aware that these changes will occur so you don't fight them. Often golfers find themselves during a particular round hitting their irons well but having trouble with the driver. Or perhaps they are driving the ball well but their iron shots are going astray. Perhaps that has happened to you. Usually that's because you relate success with your 7-iron, for example, to an upright swing motion, then try to make that same motion with your driver and get nothing but popups. You are fearful of letting your driver swing get flatter or more around your body because you don't equate that feeling with the motion that has been giving you success with your 7-iron.

So the first thing you must understand is that the swings you make with different clubs are going to feel different . . . because they *are* different. Your swing with a driver is more circular in relation to the target line, approaching the ball more from the inside and swinging back to the inside more quickly after impact. This accommodates the fact that you need more clubhead speed with the driver—remember, you can swing a club faster in a circle than in a straight line. You lose some directional control, but that's not as critical with your bigger target area. With the pitching wedge, on the other hand, the clubhead will be closer to the target line coming into and past impact and will stay on the line longer. You get more directional control and won't get the flash speed, the quick acceleration of the clubhead through impact, that you do with a longer club. That's fine. You don't want a quick burst of speed through the ball with the short irons because that can foul up your distance control, your ability to strike the ball exactly as far as you want to.

Changes in your stance line—and the way you position your body with respect to those changes—have a great influence in your swing shape and length. If you stand with your feet and body somewhat open to the target— your left foot pulled back from the line—your arms are forced to swing more back and up and you can't make as big a turn. So the open stance promotes a shorter, more upright swing, which is why it is often used with the pitching wedge, for example. If you stand a little closed to the target—your right foot pulled back from the line—you can make an easier turn away from the ball and create a longer swing that is flatter and more around your body. That's the motion you want with a driver. So deviating from the square setup position can help you make the swing you want with a particular club, as long as you are aware what those deviations are causing you to do.

The other critical factors in determining your swing shape are your posture and the distance you stand from the ball. Too many players simply will not allow themselves to stand the correct distance from the ball with the various clubs. They may feel comfortable and have success with the short irons when they are close to the ball, so they try to stand that same distance away with the driver. Or they like to stand farther away from the ball, so they are successful with the woods and longer irons but can't hit the short irons when they try to stand the same distance away.

So the distance you stand from the ball and your posture should vary with the length of the club in your hands. With the shorter irons you should be more over the ball, your spine tilted at a slightly greater angle as a result of more bend at the hips. This facilitates a more upright plane. With the longer clubs your spine will be slightly more erect, causing a flatter swing plane.

Again, you don't have to worry about consciously making these changes. They will happen automatically with each club as long as you satisfy three basic requirements:

1. The club must be properly soled, virtually flat on the ground, with the toe just slightly in the air with the longer clubs.

2. Your weight must be properly balanced toward the balls of your feet.

3. You must have the proper arm hang and extension, as we discussed earlier, hanging in a relaxed fashion and extended just enough to allow them to swing free of the body and return to the ball on an inside path.

You will find that your arms are more extended with the driver, for example, than with the pitching wedge. But this results from the difference in club length and lie. As long as you satisfy the three basic requirements, it should happen. The important thing is that you be aware that the changes will take place and that you allow them to happen instead of trying to stand to the ball in exactly the same

THE INSIDE SWING FACE-ON

position with every club.

Finally, your physique has an influence on the shape of your swing. In general, a shorter player will tend to stand more erect, especially if he is a bit heavy, and may have a flatter swing, making him better with the longer clubs than the short ones. A taller player, because he tends to get more over the ball with more spine tilt, may have a more upright swing plane and be a better iron player than he is a driver of the ball. The length of your arms is an important factor—if you have extraordinarily long arms your swing plane will tend to be flatter than that of a player with short arms.

If you notice these tendencies in your own game, you may want to make some adjustments, either in your posture or your equipment or both. Knowing the guidelines that produce the best swing shape for each particular club can help you do this.

HOW THE PARTS OF THE BODY WORK

In building a swing that approximates the model, it is important to know how the parts of the body work and specifically how *your* parts work so you may tailor your swing accordingly. Before we discuss that more fully, I want to make two points:

First, as I said, golf is a two-sided game, and the two sides must be taught to be used correctly and compatibly. If you are using a part of your body incorrectly, the cure is not to stop using it. The cure is to learn how

to use it correctly. For example, if you are making the club come down on an outside path with your right side, it is absurd to think you should try to make it come down from the inside with your left side all in one big swing change. What you must do first is learn to get the club on an inside path with the right side that is causing you all the trouble in the first place. Then at a later time, perhaps, you can let the left side become more involved. Both sides and all parts of your body must work compatibly and correctly. You cannot *consistently* compensate for one part working incorrectly by overworking another part.

In that regard, the second point I want to make is that it is vital for you to understand the relationship between the various parts of the body. The hands and wrists are linked with the feet and ankles. The arms are tied together with the legs. The shoulders are tied to the hips. Knowing this will help you coordinate the actions of your upper and lower body.

In other words, if a player is active with his hands, he should be active with his feet. If he is an active arm-swinger, he should also be active with his legs. If he is consciously trying to turn his shoulders, he should be turning his hips at the same time. If you get any of these tied-together parts working in opposition—stressing active leg-work with a passive arm swing, for example—you cannot be very consistent for very long.

In examining how you can best use

your capabilities, let me say at the beginning that the modern swing used by most of today's top players comes closest to my recommended swing model. The swing that incorporates a more lateral and vertical action, controlled by a free motion of the arms on a more down-the-line path and supported by the legs, is one I consider ideal—*if you can do it*. If you cannot, and a great many players cannot because of age, physical characteristics and the like, then you must make compensations to achieve the fullest possible motion and the free swinging of the arms that is so vital to creating clubhead speed and returning the club to the ball on an inside path.

Start with your address position. As I said earlier, the ideal setup to the ball would have all parts of your body— feet, knees, hips, shoulders, eyes— square or parallel to your target line. But if you can't return the club to the ball on an inside path, you can compensate by presetting the right side of your body inside the left side at address.

Begin with the eyes, because if you are going to develop an inside path to the ball, your eyes must let you see that inside path. Cock your chin slightly to the right, which sets your right eye inside your left eye in relation to the target line.

The ideal position at the top of the swing has the entire right side inside the left side. At impact, the right shoulder and arm still should be inside the left, although the hips and legs

have turned slightly in the opposite direction to prepare for the follow-through. If you have difficulty achieving these positions, then start by slightly closing your shoulders and hips at address, turning the right more inside the left. If you have exceptional difficulty in making a good turn, perhaps because you are thick-bodied or otherwise lack flexibility, you might even want to set your feet slightly closed, the right inside the left.

But don't get your clubface aimed and your body aligned *too far* to the right. This will give you the sensation of having to hook the ball too much to get it back to your target and eventually will promote the outside-in swing path you are trying to avoid. The ideal method is to set yourself square with the target and swing into the ball from the inside, starting it slightly to the right and curving it left, back onto the target.

In presenting my swing model, I talked about the straightness of the left arm relative to a person's flexibility and ability to produce full motion. In other words, the left arm ideally is kept relatively straight and extended throughout the backswing. (Note that I didn't say it should be kept stiff, which is what many players try to do.) But a person with less flexibility may have to let the arm bend slightly at the top to achieve a full backswing. The left arm really need not be straight anywhere other than at address and impact, especially impact. Too many players keep the left arm too straight

THE INSIDE SWING DOWN-THE-LINE

going back, reducing their range of motion and rotation, then let it bend coming forward. I would rather have the left arm bend slightly going back, allowing the player to create motion he otherwise would not have had, then let the weight and the centrifugal force created by the swinging of the club straighten and extend the arm to and through impact.

In that regard, the length of the backswing will vary with the club you are using, of course—you don't swing a 9-iron as far back as you do a driver because you are striving for more control and accuracy with the shorter clubs—and also with an individual's physical characteristics, his or her build and mobility.

With the driver, I see no reason for a person to go much beyond a 180-degree arm swing and a 90-degree hinge at the wrists, which will place the club parallel to the ground at the top. When the club goes excessively beyond parallel, the hands and the clubhead are finishing the backswing on a downward path. That means they have to move upward at the start of the forward swing. To retain the shaft-arm angle at this point requires a great deal of hand and arm strength, to say nothing of leg speed and strength.

If you are not flexible enough to swing your arms 180 degrees, and many players are not, then you must do something else to get the club parallel—hinge your hands more than 90 degrees, let your left elbow bend or make more shoulder turn. Any of this

is all right in moderation, but if you do any of it to excess you'll have problems.

There are a few things you can do to promote a longer swing if you feel it is necessary. You can release the left heel a little sooner and make the left knee work to the right a bit more. This will increase your hip and shoulder turn, which will allow the arms to swing further back. It also can reduce your tension level, which will soften your muscles and let your arms swing farther. And believe it or not, swinging slower often will let you swing your arms more fully.

But if you still can't get the club to parallel without breaking down your swing, losing your pace and going out of control, don't worry about it. Just go ahead and play with what you have. I'd much rather you put yourself in a position that is less than "full" and under control than one that is full but out of control.

Our swing model says the shoulders should follow the swinging of the arms. They should start from a square or parallel position at address, turn 90 degrees away from the target on the backswing, return to square at impact and then turn to face the target at the finish of the swing.

But the shoulders do not necessarily have to follow. A person who is thick-chested, heavily muscled in the shoulders or stiff in the upper body may have to start with his shoulders preturned, as I indicated earlier. And he may consciously have to turn the shoulders going back to increase his range of motion. If this is the case with you, be aware that the shoulders *turn*, on a plane perpendicular to the angle of your spine at address. They do not *tilt*. Trying to tilt the shoulders artificially, getting the left shoulder under the chin on the backswing and trying to keep the right shoulder under the chin on the follow-through, will create an incorrect shoulder plane and consequently an incorrect arm plane that will put you out of position.

The shoulders have a tremendous influence on your swing path back to the ball. Most of the time this is a negative influence, but it can be positive. The ultimate objective is to have the arms controlling the path of the club back to the ball, with the shoulders subservient. But if your shoulders are so dominant over your arms that they keep spinning around to an open position prior to impact, throwing your arms and the club to the outside, then you must learn to control your shoulders before you can let the arms control them.

You may want to turn your shoulders more to the right at address. You may consciously try to keep them turned longer into the forward swing. Many players who have an excessive amount of shoulder rotation to the left starting the forward swing have been helped, sometimes miraculously, by feeling as if they *increase* the shoulder turn at the start of the forward swing. This doesn't actually happen, but it slows down the unturning of the shoulders and gives the arms a chance to start down on an inside path. In effect, they are re-routing their arms and the club, but to the inside, where they should be, not to the outside.

What I have said about the shoulders also is applicable to the hips. Remember, the hips and shoulders are married. If your hips don't turn enough going away from the ball and/or turn too soon returning to the ball, you will be in trouble. Ideally, the hips should turn about 45 degrees—approximately half as much as your shoulders—on the backswing, return to square or just slightly open at impact and end up facing the target at the finish of your swing. If you are flexible, the hip turn on the backswing should come naturally as a result of the shoulders turning. But if you are thick-waisted or otherwise inflexible, you may have to work for a while at consciously turning the hips to develop the feel of them working properly.

It is just as easy to get the arms and club outside on the forward swing by spinning the hips too soon as it is by a too-quick shoulder rotation. If this is your problem, then you may have to consciously restrain the rotary action of the hips starting down to develop an arm swing that comes down from the inside. John Jacobs, the noted British teacher, is fond of saying, "Close the door with the hips." But if you get the door closed before the club gets to the ball, you are closing the door to the inside path.

Which brings us to footwork, one of

THE INSIDE SWING FROM OVERHEAD

the most underrated, misunderstood and neglected factors in the golf swing. Footwork is important for one reason—it affects what you can do with your golf swing. Or can't do. Basically, it can provide you with the motion you need in your swing and can help you use that motion correctly.

For example, it would be absurd for a person who stands 5'6", weighs 200 pounds and has a large chest and stomach to play golf flat-footed. He wouldn't have enough flexibility in his body to get any range of motion whatsoever. While that may be an extreme example, it applies to some degree to most of us whose flexibility is limited for one reason or another. By improving footwork, almost everybody can improve the action of the legs, hips, shoulders, arms and hands—everything in the swing.

Correct foot action begins at address. Your weight should favor your right foot, not your left, to a lesser extent with the short irons and to an increasingly greater extent as you go to the longer clubs.

As the club starts back and the left foot starts to react to the backswing, you should roll inward with your ankle and then upward with your heel. It's important that the left ankle roll inward, because it allows the left knee to move correctly to the right on the backswing. If the ankle remains stiff and you just lift up your left heel, the left knee will go forward. In most cases it will buckle underneath you, your shoulders will tilt, your weight will go to the left side and your swing becomes a disaster.

As you continue into your backswing and swing the club around your body, your weight transfers toward the heel area of the right foot. I would advise against letting your weight go to the outside of your right foot, because this can cause your right knee to buckle outward and make you sway so far off the ball that a lot of compensation is required to get back to the ball correctly. However, trying to keep your weight too much on the inside of your right foot, as is commonly advised, can cause the reverse weight shift to the left we discussed earlier, and that's worse than the sway. Having your weight balanced on the flat of your foot toward the heel area at the top of your swing is the goal you should seek.

Going forward, the right foot plays a vital role in controlling the path of the club. If you allow your right heel to come off the ground and rotate too quickly, you are enhancing your chances of a premature rotary action with your shoulders that will get the club coming down on an outside path. Take a swing and check your finish position—if the right heel has rotated outside the right toe, chances are you have rotated your shoulders too soon on the forward swing.

The correct action of the right foot on the forward swing is the exact opposite of the left-foot action on the backswing. Starting forward, the left

154

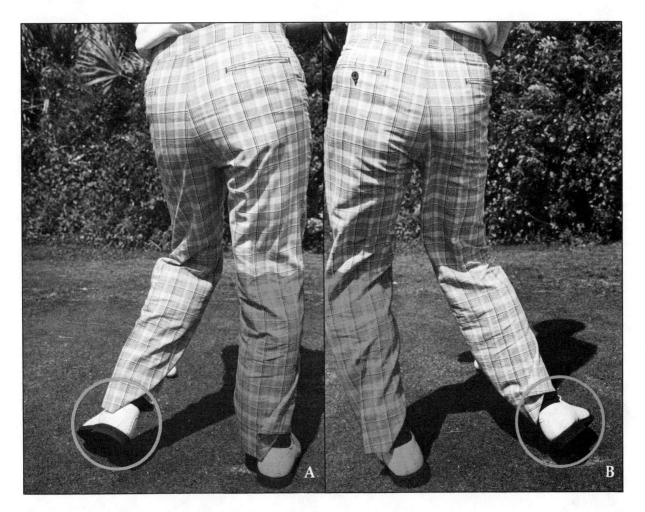

Good footwork allows weight transfer

Footwork requires heel and toe action if it is to be effective. The feet accommodate themselves to the movement of your hands. When the hands go back and around and then up behind the body, there has to be a transfer of weight and movement toward the right heel. At the top of the backswing you are on your right heel and left toe (A). The hands then start downward and inward as your weight remains momentarily on the right heel. As your hands begin to move laterally in front of your body, your weight starts to move to the left foot (B). As the hands finish around and behind your body, your weight is on the left heel with the right toe providing balance. This footwork allows the right leg to be the axis of the backswing and the left leg to be the axis of the forward swing.

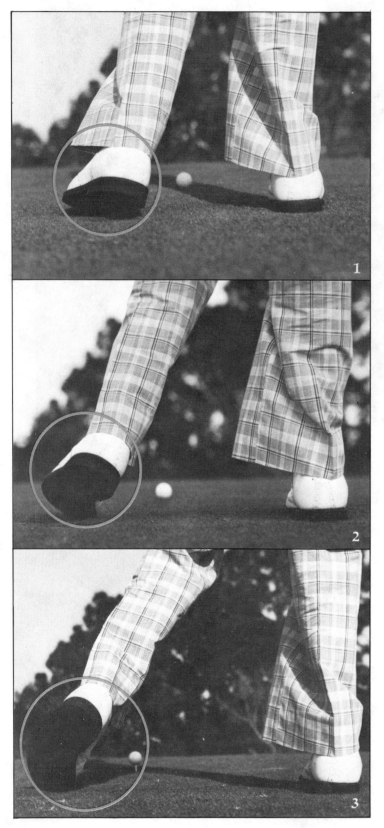

The longer your swing, the more your feet come into play

With the shorter irons, the left heel is released only slightly, but as the club and the swing become longer, the left heel comes more and more off the ground on the backswing.

1

2

3

heel is replanted and your weight begins to roll from the flat of the foot to the outside and from toe to heel as you swing around into your follow-through. Simultaneously, the right ankle rolls inward, the weight going to the inside of your right foot and from the heel toward the toe until finally the heel is released from the ground. With all clubs except perhaps the driver, where you are making an unusually full, hard swing, the inside of your foot should still be on the ground at impact.

After impact, when the club starts to move around your body to the left, your right heel releases to accommodate that follow-through motion. If you push off your right heel too soon on the forward swing, you will throw the right side of your body outside the left, creating a rotary action that brings the club down on an outside path.

If you are relaxed and flexible and doing everything else correctly in your swing, your footwork may be reflexively correct. If this is not the case, and it probably isn't, you will need to consciously practice your footwork until you develop the proper habits and sensation.

When we discussed the development of your swing in Part II, you learned that the hands are the key to success with the upper body and the feet are the keys to success with the lower body. You develop your golf swing from the hands up and from the feet up.

CHAPTER · 8

HOW THE SHORT SHOTS RELATE TO THE FULL SWING

I could not honestly publish a book entitled "The Inside Path to Better Golf" without tying in the short game, an area which is so vital in producing better scores. In this case the tie-in is easy. I believe, contrary to some opinions, that the short shots are struck exactly the same way as the full shots—from the inside and with the hands controlling the swing.

So once you have progressed through the full-swing stages, you should be accomplished in the short game as well. Most off-green short shots are made simply with Stage I and Stage II swings. Only as you approach full-swing distance for a normal pitch shot would you advance to Stage III, and I can't think of an instance when you would ever want to employ a Stage IV swing with a short iron in your hands. Control, not maximum distance, becomes critical as you move closer to the green.

Most higher-handicap golfers make the same mistake with the short shots that they do with the full ones. Because they use their hands incorrectly, they try to eliminate them and so become much too arm- and shoulder-oriented. And you never really can eliminate the hands from most swings, no matter how short. They will instinctively jump into action, usually at the wrong time.

This becomes especially damaging in the short shots, where the margin of error is so much less and the need for feel and sensitivity is so great. So you must learn to trust your hands as friends, not suspect them as enemies. Train them to work properly to control the arms, which in turn control the shoulders.

Accomplishing this will promote confidence, reduce tension and allow you to develop the softness in your hands and arms that will give you the magical touch so necessary to reducing strokes around the green.

In the remainder of this chapter I will quickly review the short-game swings with respect to the stages of learning, then will give you a method that will clarify and simplify your concept of playing all the short shots.

THE BASIC SHORT SHOTS

Let's first discuss the basic swing-shape difference between the good and bad short-game players. Bad short-game players, either by design or by result, cannot create the proper descending blow. Their backswings tend to be more down and around and their forward swings finish up. They scoop or top their short shots with an early release of the hands. The good players have backswings that are more up and less around, forward swings that are more down, with a later release of the hands that gives them a descending blow and crisper, more controlled shots.

With that correct shape in mind, let's examine the swings you will need for the short shots, from the shortest to the longest.

For shots from just off the putting surface, when distance is not a problem, your best choice may be to chip with a one-lever putting stroke. You may use any lofted club, depending on how far the ball must carry and how far it can roll. But I would rarely use any club longer than a 4-iron. Make a pendulum-type stroke with your arms only, striking the ball at the bottom of your arc or just slightly on the descent. Keep your hands and wrists relatively firm, with no hinging during the stroke. If you wish, you may use your putting grip—which I'll describe later in this section—to help stabilize your hands and arms.

You don't have as much distance potential with this stroke, but with practice your accuracy and control can be better.

When the shot gets too long for the one-lever stroke—and you'll have to experiment to find out just how long that is for the greens you are playing—you must go to the two-lever system.

Here the underlying principle is that if you are going to use your hands and set an angle between the shaft and your arms, you want to do it as soon as possible so you can retain it longer throughout the swing. The sequence is the same as in the full-swing stages—hands-arms going back, arms-hands coming forward.

For a little chip shot, simply cock your hands upward and inward and tap downward. Feel familiar? That's the first little swing in Stage I, except that because you are just trying to tap the club downward into the back of the ball you need not worry about re-forming the angle after impact. The force of the blow dissipates into the ground as the left hand and wrist stabilize the stroke.

As the shot becomes longer and the need for motion increases, you simply cock your hands more fully. You won't need an appreciable arm swing until you approach a full cocking of

Short shots are inside-to-inside, too

Even the shortest shots follow the same stroke
principle—from the inside on the forward swing and back to
the inside on the follow-through.

Clubhead feels "up" going back, lower going forward

For good short-game play, you must develop the feeling that the clubhead moves more back and up in the backswing while staying lower in the follow-through.

162

your hands. Then swing your arms more and more as you need distance. If you start with your arms first, then get your hands into action, you will end up with too big a swing for the shot you are facing. This instinctively will lead to deceleration on the forward swing.

Always retain the hands-arms, arms-hands sequence. As your stroke becomes longer with the more-lofted clubs, you will begin to re-form the angle after impact, just as you do with the full-shot swings.

The short shots are made almost entirely with the hands and the arms. The function of the lower body is to provide support and traction. However, this does not mean your legs should be static, nor should you restrict your body from pivoting. The legs should be relatively still on the backswing, because the need on the short swing is to get the club more up and less around. But they should be free to move on the forward swing to provide support, just as they do on the full swing. They just won't move as much or as quickly, because the force of the arm swing is so much less.

The concept that will let your short-game swing work most efficiently is one I call the "vertical-line method." That simply means your swing center, your hands and your center of gravity should be in a vertical line at address, when viewed from face-on or above. Your swing center is a point in the middle of your sternum or breastbone. Your center of gravity is, in effect, the centerpoint of your weight distribution. To establish the vertical line, your hands should be directly under your swing center and your weight should be centered directly under your hands.

The position of the vertical line in relation to the ball then determines your shot trajectory with a particular club. The farther ahead of the ball your vertical line is set, the more you de-loft the club and the lower the shot you will get. The farther behind the ball you position the vertical line, the more effective loft you add to the club and the higher your shot will fly.

The most important factor in setting your vertical line is ball position. You must first preset your hands in relation to the ball, then place your feet accordingly. Don't position your feet first, then decide you want the vertical line way to the left. You will either fall over or fail to get the low shot you want.

Most shots can be played from the neutral position, the vertical line even with the ball. If you want to hit the ball lower than normal, just set your hands ahead of the ball and line up your swing center and center of gravity accordingly. Rarely should your vertical line be behind or to the right of the ball, but if you have to hit a high, soft lob you may have to put it there. Then it becomes especially important to have the vertical factors in line. If your hands are out of whack with your swing center and weight placement, you are courting disaster in

Distance of shot determines length of swing

The distance to the target dictates the length of backswing you need for any given short shot. The longer the shot, the more fully the hands hinge and the longer the arms swing. Regardless of the length, always try to maintain the sequence of hands first, arms second in the backswing.

terms of topped shots or striking the ground behind the ball. If you make a swing mistake with your vertical line established, you have a much better chance of still making clean contact with the descending blow you need.

All your short shots should be played with an open stance, your left foot pulled farther back from the target line than your right. A stance line that is 45 degrees open to the target line is a good guideline, but you can experiment to find what is comfortable for you.

The open stance enhances the swing shape you want. It will allow your club to work more backward and upward, whereas a square or closed

stance will induce a backswing plane that is more back and around. An open stance also encourages the freer leg movement you need on the forward swing.

Most important, presetting your stance line and your vertical line allows you to swing on the inside path. You don't have to pick the club up or take it outside to "cut" the ball or make any special shot. You don't have to change the path of your swing in any way to change the shape or trajectory of your shot. With both swing shape and shot trajectory predetermined, all you have to do is swing your hands and arms in normal fashion.

Once you set your stance and your vertical line, the only other factor in determining trajectory and distance for most shots is *club selection*. Assuming you can make a normal swing, the selection of your club should be based on the theory of *minimum air time, maximum ground time*. That means you should land the ball on the putting surface as quickly as possible and let it roll as far as possible to the hole. That's because you have more control by rolling the ball than by pitching it close to the hole and subjecting it to differences in green hardness and spin factors, whether the ball checks or runs after it lands.

If your ball is close to the putting

surface and you have quite a distance to go to the hole, you may want to use a medium-lofted iron such as a 4, 5, 6 or 7. But if you have to pitch over a bunker and the hole is cut close to the near edge of the green, you may need to use a sand wedge.

Your club selection—as well as the positioning of the vertical line—for all shots should be determined by practice, so that when you are faced with a situation you will know by experience how you want to handle it. The one warning I would make is that I see most players using clubs with too-little loft and making too short a swing, try-ing to add loft to the club with their hands by scooping and so ruining the shot. If you are going to make a mistake in club selection or swing, my preference would be for you to select a club with more loft than necessary, de-loft it a bit and make a longer swing than necessary, dissipating the force in-to the ground.

In a nutshell or two, that's all you have to worry about in the short game. Aim the club, preset the trajec-tory of your shot by club selection and positioning the vertical line, then think only of the length and pace of your swing, creating sufficient hand and

Vertical line determines trajectory of shot

The way you set the vertical line—your swing center, hands and center of gravity—dictates the trajectory of your shot. If the line is set behind the ball (A), you will get a high trajectory; if it is even with the ball (B), a normal trajectory; if it is in front of the ball (C), a low trajectory; and if it is well in front (D), the lowest possible trajectory with any given club.

How your blade position influences flight pattern

These pictures show the ball flights that result from various blade positions through impact. If you hold the blade open by not rotating the hands (A), you get a higher, softer shot that travels slightly to the right and rolls less upon landing. With the blade square (B), you get a straight shot with normal trajectory for the club you're using. If you rotate the blade closed (C), you get a lower shot that goes slightly left and rolls farther after landing.

arm motion to negotiate the distance you want.

Again, practice is necessary to determine just what swing length and speed is necessary with each particular club to send the ball the required distance. There is no other shortcut to short-game success.

Once you have developed proficiency with the basic shots, you can further refine your short game by influencing your ball flight with your hand and arm rotation. Because you are controlling your swing with your hands in the first place and because you are always swinging on the basic inside path, this is not difficult to do with sufficient practice.

You have three options—square up the blade at impact with normal rotation to produce the shot your address position has dictated; delay rotation to produce a higher ball flight; increase rotation to produce a lower ball flight.

For example, if you have a down-wind shot to a close-cut flag, you may want to hold the blade more open through impact and get a higher, softer-landing shot. Into the wind, or when you face a long, uphill chip, turning the blade over by increasing your hand and arm rotation will give you a lower, hotter shot that will roll faster.

When you leave the clubface open the ball will slide a little to the right, and when you turn the blade over the ball will go a bit left, so adjust your aim for these tendencies.

Having incorporated this additional weapon, your short-game arsenal as far as the basic shots are concerned is now complete.

THE SAND SHOTS

Whereas most professional golfers probably would rather be in a sand trap than anywhere else around the green, most amateurs have a deathly fear of the stuff. That's because they have failed so often at getting out of bunkers.

That failure almost always is due to an improper concept of how to get a ball out of a bunker and close to the hole. They think they have to do something special, and this leads to an improper setup and improper use of the hands and arms. They think they have to swing outside-in and "cut" the shot, consciously hit behind the ball, whatever. The result usually is disaster, which creates the fear, which compounds the disaster next time.

To give you the proper concept of bunker play, and to rid you of that fear, I want to suggest a four-point approach that will let you use the normal swing you have developed through the stages of learning, incorporating the inside-to-inside path and the two-lever action that you use for every other shot.

This four-step program addresses itself to the basic problem that most players have with the sand shot—the club never touches the ball. Now the player is trying to displace a quantity

Sand play: Make ball fly out on cushion of sand

The most important point to understand when playing greenside bunker shots is that the ball is carried out on a cushion of sand—the club displaces the sand and the sand displaces the ball.

of sand which will carry out the golf ball as just another grain of sand.

To do that you must solve these four problems:

1. How to get the club to enter the sand behind the ball.

2. How to get the club to go under the ball and displace the proper amount of sand consistently.

3. How to get the sand—and the ball—to go in the right direction consistently.

4. How to get the sand and the ball to go the right distance.

The solutions, then, in order:

1. To get the club to enter the sand behind the ball.

You spend most of your golfing life with your feet on the ground and a ball at the base of your feet. You relate to your swing center being a certain distance from the ball, and hopefully you learn to strike the ball first and the ground second.

Now, suddenly, you are going to make a swing that is designed to strike several inches behind the ball, something you have been trying to avoid all the time you have been learning to play golf. What happens is that you *try* to hit behind the ball, so you get a premature release of the hands, an outside-to-inside movement of the hands that brings the club down from the outside. You probably are compounding the problem because somebody has told you to aim the clubface right, set your body left, swing left and watch the ball go straight. What you end up with in any event is an outside path to the ball.

Here is the simplest way in the world to overcome those problems. To insure that the club strikes the sand behind the ball—*lower your swing center.* In other words, if the ball is on turf and the bottoms of your feet are level with the bottom of your ball, you will strike the ball first because that is the way your swing has been developed. So if you are in a bunker, simply work your feet into the sand until they are below the bottom of your ball. Don't choke down on the club. Hold the clubhead above the sand because you aren't allowed to ground the club until the forward swing. Now just make your normal swing and try to hit the ball. You won't. Your arms will extend naturally and you will strike the sand behind the ball, because you have lowered your swing center, which lowered the arc of your swing.

You can do this for 90 percent or more of the shots you face. In those odd situations when you are standing outside of the bunker or are facing a really bad lie, it becomes a matter of sensitivity and feel, of eye-hand coordination. You must bend your knees or bend more from the hips or whatever you can do to lower your swing center.

Don't worry about having to strike the sand a certain distance behind the ball. The old saw about hitting an inch or two inches back of the ball is strictly a myth. You have a great deal more margin for error with the shot than you would think, which is why you really don't need to fear it. Striking anywhere from two to six inches behind the ball usually will give you a satisfactory result if you use the bounce of your club and your angle of attack correctly. You'll learn about that next.

So the first rule is—don't *try* to hit behind the ball. Accomplish it simply by lowering your swing center.

2. To get the club to go under the ball and consistently displace the right amount of sand.

Regulating how far into the sand the club goes is determined by your club-face position, which is determined by your lie. You want the clubface passing far enough under the ball that there is no club-ball contact. But you don't need to get under it more than half an inch or so. With that in mind, let's first examine your sand wedge. You'll notice it has a curved sole or flange that usually extends below the leading edge of the club. This causes the club to "bounce" or skid *through* the sand instead of digging *into* it. How much it skids and how thin the resulting cut of sand you take depends on how much you bring the sole or bounce into play. The more you open the clubface, the more bounce you get and the less sand you displace. The more you square the clubface, the deeper the club will dig and the more sand you will take.

So, with a normal lie, the ball sitting up reasonably nicely in the sand, you simply set the blade open, dig in your

Sand play: Set clubface to regulate depth of cut

To regulate the depth of cut in the sand, preset the clubface according to the lie. For a normal lie (A), set the blade open; for a fair lie (B), set it square or slightly closed; and for a buried lie (C), set the blade closed.

feet below the level of the ball and try to hit the ball. The club will skid through the sand and under the ball, which will come out as just another grain.

If the ball is buried, you set the blade square or closed, dig your feet in below the bottom of the ball and try to hit the ball. Because the club will dig deeper into the sand, it will cut under the buried ball and send it flying out.

So just by positioning your feet and the clubface you can get the ball out of the sand with your normal swing. You must learn through experimentation and practice how much to adjust your blade position to accommodate various lies and different consistencies of sand. In general, the heavier and wetter the sand, the less bounce you want. The drier and finer the sand, the more bounce you need.

3. How to get the sand and ball to go in the right direction consistently.

This one is easy. The clubface has no influence on the direction of the ball because the clubface is not hitting the ball. The only thing that influences where the ball goes is the direction in which you displace the sand.

That outside-in swing can be a culprit again in ruining your directional control. Try this experiment for me. Without a ball, make a swing in the bunker and explode a cut of sand. Notice that the sand spreads right and left as it flies—the sand that was displaced by the toe sails to the right, that displaced by the heel goes left. The sand displaced by the middle of

Sand play: Ball flies in same direction as sand

The direction in which you displace the sand that is under the ball also will be the direction the ball travels.

173

the club flew straight, so you obviously want your ball to be among those particles.

The problem with the outside-in swing is that too often you get only the toe of the club passing underneath the ball, which means the ball will sail to the right of where you are aiming. And, of course, if you get the heel passing too much under the ball, you're liable to shank it.

So it's vitally important to get the middle of the club passing underneath the ball on the line on which you want the ball to fly. You do this simply by setting up with an open stance, as you do for the other short shots, but still swinging from the inside and down the line toward the target. Don't be concerned that your clubface is open, square or closed. *Direction is determined solely by your swing path,* and you get that path going to the target by making your normal inside swing.

4. To get the ball to go the right distance.

Distance from the sand is controlled by the length and speed of your swing motion and by the trajectory of your shot. Remember that trajectory is determined by your angle of approach—the ball will come out of the sand at the same angle the club enters it. Consequently, the more V-shaped your swing and the steeper your angle of approach, the higher and shorter the ball will fly. The wider and more U-shaped your swing and the shallower your angle of approach, the lower and longer the ball will travel.

Thus you have three basic methods for determining the distance of your shots. The first, and the one you will use probably 75 percent of the time, is simply to set up normally, your weight favoring your left side a bit, your stance open and your vertical line—swing center, hands and weight distribution—set just slightly ahead of the ball. You should be almost in a neutral position. Then just vary your distance with the length and speed of your arm swing. If you want the ball to go farther, make a longer swing; not as far, a shorter swing. Remember at all times, however, to make your swing long enough to compensate for the deadening effect of the sand. Your shots won't go as far with the same length swing as they would if you were playing them off grass, so take this into account and use a longer motion. Again, experimentation and practice will give you a feel for how long and fast a swing you need for various distances.

Now, if you want the ball to come out higher and shorter—if you absolutely cannot afford to have the ball go over the green because there is an out-of-bounds line or a lake there, if you need to pop it over a steep bank or obviously if you have a plugged lie—you turn to your V-shaped swing.

Begin by gripping the club more in your fingers, which will allow you to pick it up more abruptly. Open your stance more and set your weight more to the left, your vertical line farther ahead of the ball. Don't forget to dig

Sand play: How address influences
shot trajectory

Different weight distribution at address creates different
trajectories on shots from sand, the opposite of those off
grass. Normal address, with the weight set slightly left (A),
produces a normal trajectory. The weight set right (B) gives
you a lower and longer trajectory, and the weight set well to
the left (C) results in a shot that flies higher and shorter.

your feet in below the bottom of the bottom. All this will create the more up-and-down swing with a steeper angle of approach that will bring the ball out higher and shorter.

For the extra-long bunker shots—a 40- or 50-yard shot, for example—you need an especially shallow angle of approach. The best way to do this is to make sure the club is approaching from the inside. So close your stance, which causes you to swing the club more around your body and insures that it approaches on the shallow angle you want. Again, the ball will travel in the direction of your swing path, so adjust your aim accordingly.

Within those three guidelines you can make the adjustments in length

and speed of motion and angle of approach that will let you succeed in virtually every bunker shot you will ever encounter. By applying the principles that affect the distance and direction of the ball, you can handle all types of slopes, unusual lies and sand texture.

A word about spinning the ball out of the sand—under most circumstances, *don't*, at least until you develop great proficiency. To get a lot of spin on the ball out of a bunker you must get the sand nearest the ball moving quickly, which means you must get the clubface moving quickly and take a minimum amount of sand under the ball. This requires good hand action and great precision. The slightest mis-swing can cause you to blade the ball

Sand play: Bunker swing more vertical

The plane of the swing in the bunker will be slightly more upright than normal—as in the "tee drill," the butt end of the club will point inside the line of play. This is a result of your slightly open stance line. But remember that the basic shape of the swing remains inside-to-inside.

and send it flying far over the green. And when you are relying on spin to stop the ball you always are subject to the vagaries of green surface. You might strike the shot perfectly, but if the ball lands on a hard spot it won't check and will roll far past the hole.

You are much safer trying to stop the ball with trajectory, taking a little more sand and letting the ball land softly and roll to the target.

Finally—or perhaps primarily—to be a successful sand player you must *prepare* properly and *swing* properly. To prepare, plant your feet very precisely, setting the target side of both feet lower in the sand and setting the balls of your feet lower than the heels, your weight distributed according to the type of shot you want to play. The worst thing I see players doing in the bunker is digging in their heels, which puts their weight back, their spines up and causes them to throw the club from the top.

Once you are correctly set, your swing is simply one of those you have learned in the stages of development. The shorter shots can be played with perhaps a Stage II or the beginning of Stage III swings, basically with the hands and arms. But when the length of your arm swing becomes at all significant, you must remember the rule that applies to all shots—your legs must support the swinging of your arms.

Don't be afraid to let your lower body move on bunker shots, because that movement allows you to maintain the inside path of the golf swing. If your legs become stagnant, you will tend to release the club with a rotary action of your upper body, spinning the club to the outside and cutting across the ball too much or even shanking it. So to be as consistent as you should be, let your legs move to support your arm swing.

THE PUTTING STROKES AND HOW TO MAKE THEM WORK

Before we get into the basic putting stroke and its variations, let's briefly discuss the putting grip and your setup to the ball.

The grip is intended to stabilize the hands and arms and promote a one-lever action, at least for the shorter strokes. The club should be held in the palm and against the heel pad of the left hand, basically resting against the lifeline. It should be held more in the fingers of the right hand. The hands should be facing or perhaps a bit opposed, the left hand turned to the left the same amount that the right hand is turned to the right.

Within those guidelines, you may utilize the normal reverse overlap putting grip, in which the left forefinger overlaps the fingers of the right hand, or the double overlap, in which the left forefinger overlaps the right hand fingers and the little finger of the right overlaps the middle finger of the left. The latter grip brings the hands closer together and serves to unify their action. Or you may use your regular full-swing grip. The variations are matters

177

of personal choice, so long as your grip satisfies the basic purpose.

The stabilization of the hands and forearms is necessary, I feel, for the basic short putt, which ideally should be made with a one-lever stroke. For longer putts, your stroke and your grip may have to vary.

Your setup is basically a matter of keeping everything balanced. Your weight should be distributed evenly between right and left and toward the centers of your feet. The blow on the ball should be level, which means you should position the ball somewhere close to the center or slightly forward of the center of your stance.

I am not as adamant as some are about your eyes being squarely over the target line, simply because there are too many good putters whose eyes are not directly over that line. As far as I'm concerned, your eyes can be set over the target line or inside the line, because that still will accommodate the stroke you will be making. I would not recommend positioning your eyes outside the line, because that can adversely affect your aim and stroke.

It *is* important, when setting up, to make sure your shoulders are square or parallel to the target line and your forearms are set parallel to that line. I also prefer that your forearms be on the same plane as the putter shaft, matching the angle of the shaft to the ground.

The point you must understand from the beginning is that *the putting stroke is just a smaller version of your full golf swing.* The only variation from that concept is the one-lever system for the very shortest putts, those within six feet or so, depending on the speed of the green. For the short stroke, your grip is a bit firmer, your hands and arms work as a unit and the putterhead never comes off the target line, back or through. There is more acceleration coming forward than in the more pendulum-like action of the longer stroke.

Once you get outside that short range, you must dispel the myths of keeping the putter low and on line. It just doesn't happen that way in the longer strokes. Every good putter I have ever seen strikes the ball from the inside, letting the blade turn over as it moves back to the inside on the follow-through, just as in the full swing.

I have never seen a good putter who strikes the golf ball from the outside or who works the blade from shut to open. As the stroke gets longer, the putterhead must work inside and up on the backswing, back level and on-line at impact, then inside and up again on the follow-through. The blade opens to the line going back, squares at impact and closes again on the follow-through. So the entire action is similar to that of your regular full shot.

The putting motion is controlled by your hands and arms. The amount of hinging at the wrists and rotation of your arms and blade can be controlled to a great extent by your grip, which is why I advocate a short-putt grip and a long-putt grip.

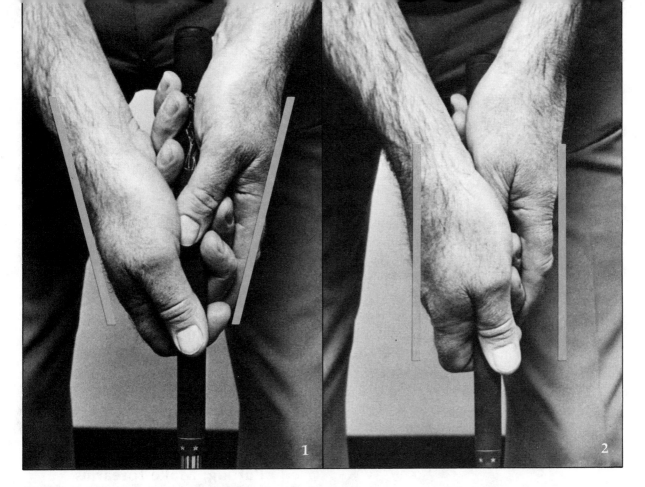

Putting: Grip varies with distance of putt

Your two basic putting grips should have the hands opposed (left) for shorter putts and in a more neutral or palms-facing position (right) for longer putts in which more hand action is needed.

The short-putt grip is formed by setting the hands more in opposition, the left hand turned more under the shaft and the right hand turned under an equal amount. This grip restricts wrist action and helps eliminate unwanted flash speed. You still are controlling the stroke with your hands and arms, but now the action of both is tied together, your arms supporting the movement of your hands with no hinging at the wrist.

In combination with this one-lever stroke you will want a slight increase in grip pressure. This will further inhibit hinging at the wrists and will help you keep the blade on line better. The firmer grip may make you less sensitive in controlling distance, but distance control is not so critical on the short putts.

As the putts get longer, your grip should change from opposing to more neutral, the palms more facing each other. As this happens, the handle of the putter also moves a bit more toward the fingers, resting more against the heel pad of the left hand instead of directly along the lifeline. Your hands will be set a little lower, with less arching at the wrists. Your grip pressure also should lighten a bit. The more neutral hand position and lighter pressure allows hinging at the

Putting: Make forearms parallel extensions of shaft

At address, your shoulders and both forearms should be set on a line parallel to the target line. Your forearms also should hang on the same plane as the puttershaft, matching the angle of the shaft to the ground.

The putting stroke is inside-to-inside

For other than the very short putts, the path of the putting stroke should be inside-to-inside, the same as for every other shot.

wrists, which gives you a better feel for distance and the leverage you need for longer putts. If you tried to hit a 60- or 70-foot putt with a one-lever system, your stroke would have to be four feet long.

I can't tell you exactly when you should change from a short-putt to a long-putt grip. That depends not only on the distance of the putt but the speed of the green. If the greens you play on are particularly quick, you might be able to stay with the one-lever stroke at all times. The point at which the one-lever stroke becomes awkward, when it begins to inhibit the

natural hinging and rotation that you want with a longer stroke, is when you should begin modifying your grip.

To better judge when and how much to modify your grip and stroke, divide the green into three zones— green, yellow and red. The circumference of the zones will depend to an extent on the speed of the green and your ability. As a guideline, the green zone is anything inside six feet, the yellow zone extends to 25 or 30 feet around the cup and the red zone is anything outside that.

The green zone means *go*. You are trying to make every putt within this zone. You should use an opposition grip with reasonably firm pressure and the one-lever stroke. If anything, your backswing should be shorter, your acceleration on the forward stroke greater and your follow-through longer. Basically, green-zone putts are aimed within the cup, unless you face an exceptionally severe break or other extenuating circumstances. Your concern is not distance but direction. All you want to do is get the ball to the hole on the right line.

The yellow zone means *caution*. You are trying to make the putt but you also are being careful to leave it reasonably close to the hole if you miss. In this zone your grip should still be in opposition but less so. Your stroke will be a combination of one-lever with a little angle forming, depending on the length of the putt. Your stroke is more pendulum-like, a rhythmic backward and forward movement in which the length of the backswing and follow-through are reasonably equal. There is acceleration on the forward stroke, but it is not as forceful as on the short putt.

In the red zone, *danger* looms. Your objective now is just to get the ball into the green zone. From this distance, the grip is definitely neutral and more in the fingers. The stroke is longer and with less purposeful acceleration. It is done more with the hands, hinging at the wrists as the arms swing back. Simply set the angle going back and let the weight of the putterhead swing into the ball on the forward stroke. It is almost a chipping stroke, very much like the Stage I swing you learned earlier. With practice, this type of stroke will give you much greater sensitivity and the feel for distance that is so important. Accuracy is not the issue—it's unlikely you are going to strike the putt off-line more than two or three feet. Your first objective is to stop the ball within a few feet of the hole on one side or the other.

If you have an extremely long putt and have to hit it excessively hard—perhaps 70 to 100 feet or more depending on the green speed—you may want to forget all about the putting rules and *chip* the ball with your putter. Use your regular grip, choke down on the club so the toe of the blade won't stick quite so far in the air and control the stroke with your hands. A two-lever stroke definitely is required, so set the angle early to get as much leverage as possible and just tap down, as you would on a chip shot. This allows you to hit the ball farther with less effort, so you have better control of direction and—most important—distance.

You must exercise good judgment in deciding when and where—or if—to use this stroke. Certainly I'd recommend you practice it before trying it in actual play. But being aware of its advantages can give you the full complement of strokes on the green.

CHAPTER · 9

LAST WORD ON THE INSIDE PATH

The purpose of this book has been threefold. The first objective has been to help you learn a technically correct golf swing, one created from the correct address position and with the proper muscles. The concept of swinging on an inside path and creating speed with a relatively effortless motion has been laid out in a format that gives you a quick reference to the various areas of grip, preparation and swing development.

Refer to them you must. As I indicated at the beginning of this book, nothing good ever comes quickly or easily. To unlearn old habits and ingrain new ones takes time and patience. You will progress, then regress before you progress again. If you are having problems with concept in a particular part of your swing, re-read the chapter that deals with that part. If you are having trouble executing properly, go back through the stages of development until you find one that works,

then go forward from there.

The second objective has been to help you choose a swing pattern that works for *you*, developing a technique that best utilizes your talents, your physical attributes and the time you have to devote. With the knowledge you now have of how the parts of the body work, and especially how *your* parts work, you can break out of the stereotype. You don't have to look like Jack Nicklaus. You can look like yourself and be effective.

The final and perhaps most important goal has been to heighten your *awareness*, to help you understand that you must use your imagination and not be so hidebound by myths that you inhibit your flexibility. An example is the variety of putting strokes we discussed in the previous chapter. Just as there is more than one effective putting stroke, there is more than one golf swing that can be used in different situations. The ability to adjust your swing to different situations marks the difference between a fair player and a very good player.

By understanding the ball-flight factors and cause-and-effect in the swing, you can adapt your swing to meet the different situations you will face during a round. First you must learn to recognize the situation. That involves not only trouble shots and how best to perform them but your normal shots in the course of play—your success with the driver while having trouble with your irons during a round, for example. Remember what I said about swing shapes? Being aware of your tendencies, good and bad, and what you can do to correct your problems between the first tee and the 18th green is a big part of *awareness*.

Recognizing the situation, of course, is of no value unless you possess the ability, the technique, to do something about it. If you don't, sooner or later you will lose the recognition factor because you won't be able to react to it.

So practice your technique and its variations. By improving this aspect of your game you will become more attuned to applying your acquired skills and will more readily recognize the circumstances in which they are applicable.

With the successful tour players it all happens instinctively. They see, they analyze and they react with the swing they know they can make to hit the shot they must execute. They don't concern themselves with technical thoughts at the moment. For them it has become a matter of feel.

Frankly, you have to work a long time to earn the right to be able to play with feel rather than mechanical thoughts. But the beautiful thing about the game of golf is that everything is relative, that improvement comes by degrees. We are not necessarily measured by the games we win or lose but by the strokes we record for each round. And the closer you can come to playing by feel, the sharper you can make your awareness, for however few shots a round, the more strokes you are going to cut from your score each time out.

The more you see that happening, the more you are fulfilling the objectives of this book and the closer you are coming to fulfilling your potential as a golfer. Whether you ever reach your ultimate potential is up to you. It is dependent on the amount of time and effort you put into the search. But in the meantime you're going to have a lot more fun trying for it.